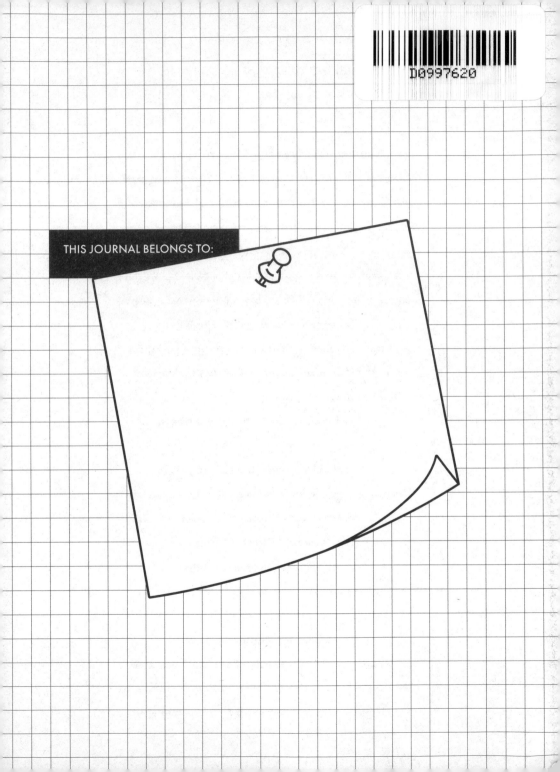

THIS JOURNAL BELONGS TO:

PRAISE FOR *SLAY IN YOUR LANE*:

Winners of the **Groucho Maverick Award**

Winners of the **Marie Claire Future Shapers Award**

Shortlisted for the **Specsavers National Book Award**

Shortlisted for the **British Book Awards Non-Fiction Lifestyle Book of the Year**

'A comprehensive, inspirational tool book that gives voice to the next generation of young black British women' **Vogue**

'Everyone should read it' **Sadiq Khan**

'A brilliant insight into being a black woman in Britain' **Otegha Uwagba, author of Little Black Book**

'Offers wisdom and encouragement to a rising generation of black female leaders' **Sheryl Sandberg**

'Inspirational' **Elle**

'A cultural landmark' **Daily Telegraph**

'This book will have a profound impact on the way we discuss race and women' **Dolly Alderton**

'Fantastic' **Diane Abbott**

'Stylish, sassy and funny' **Metro**

'A prime example of how straightforward it should be to provide representation for young black girls' **Vice**

'Magnificent' **Emma Gannon**

'A super-smart, exuberant manifesto' **ES Magazine**

'These two remarkable women took the kickass step of writing their own rulebook' **Deborah Frances-White**

YOMI ADEGOKE is a multi-award-winning journalist and author. She has worked at ITN, Channel 4 News and is the women's columnist at the Guardian. She has also freelanced for Vogue, Elle, and the Independent amongst others. Last year she was listed as one of the most influential people in London by the Evening Standard. She was awarded Journalist of the Year in 2018 by the Woman In Africa awards.

ELIZABETH UVIEBINENÉ is an award-winning marketing manager and strategist. She previously worked in the City for a global brand producing campaigns that spark conversations and stay ahead of the curve. Last year, she was recognised by The Dots as a woman 'Redefining the Creative Industry', awarded a Rising Star in the PR, Communication and Marketing Industry by WeAreTheCity and listed as one of the most influential people in London by the Evening Standard.

4th Estate

An imprint of HarperCollinsPublishers

1 London Bridge Street

London SE1 9GF

www.4thEstate.co.uk

First published in Great Britain in 2019 by 4th Estate

1

Designed and illustrated by Sherida Kuffour

A catalogue record for this book is available from the British Library

ISBN 978-0-00-834260-9

Set in Futura Medium and Bluu Suuperstar

Printed and bound by CPI Group (UK) Ltd, Croydon, CR0 4YY

SLAY IN YOUR LANE:

YOMI ADEGOKE AND ELIZABETH UVIEBINENÉ

In *Slay In Your Lane* we spoke to 39 of the most trailblazing black women in Britain and painted a picture of what it means to be a black British girl at this moment in time (the good and the bad). We looked at the triumphs and the challenges, the hurdles we need to overcome and the way those hurdles are being vaulted over. We covered everything from mental health to physical health, careers, entrepreneurship and even dating!

In that book, and in this journal, we are not trying to tell you that if you simply go for gold, put your mind to it and believe, you can slay yourself out of systemic racism.

Our aim with *Slay In Your Lane* was to start a movement that would amplify the voices and increase the visibility of black women who have been made thoroughly invisible by the mainstream. We had high hopes for the book, but even we didn't expect it to be the phenomenon it has become. It sparked a great many conversations over the summer of 2018 and on into 2019, and over the course of just a few months we spoke at nearly 50 events, from City Hall in London, to bookshops in Edinburgh, from Croydon Box Park to a primary school in Hackney, from Amazon's head office in Luxembourg, to a pod in the London Eye for the Women of the World Festival. We have spoken to over 5,000 of you so far, and the conversations show no sign of drying up...

But at every event, the same questions would crop up again and again: how did we manage to write the book and work full time? How did we get the women we interviewed to talk to us? And above all, what practical advice could we give about how we have managed to slay in our own lanes?

In this journal we distil the answers to those questions, and the many others raised by *Slay In Your Lane*, into inspirational tips and hints, and suggest practical ways to help you create a better, more visible future for yourself.

And, like *Slay In Your Lane*, we hope this journal will offer you encouragement and inspiration, but also, most importantly, some practical support. The activities in the pages that follow are designed to help you take charge of all areas of your life, to give you the tools and the confidence to be in the driving seat and not just a passenger. They may require you to step outside your comfort zone, both personally and professionally, but as the saying goes, 'A comfort zone is a beautiful place, but nothing ever grows there.' Outside this zone the opportunities to grow and learn are limitless.

We will be covering topics from health to relationships, to personal finance, to higher education, to your own personal brand, to activism and entrepreneurialism – offering advice and tips on how you can start slaying in your own lane in everything you do.

We want to help you tap into your unique skills and unearth your passions. This journal experience is your opportunity to learn more about yourself. In order to get the most out of this, dedicate some time to completing the different sections. It will require you to dig deep and reflect on how you've come to be who you are and where you'd like to go in the future. We hope this journal will help you track the amazing things you've achieved already, to identify new areas for growth and to help you spot, and avoid, the roadblocks ahead that might prevent you from reaching your goals.

Before you start, take a moment to think about what you'd like to get out of this journal. What are you looking forward to learning or taking away from this experience? Write it down now so you can come back to it at the end and see how far you've come:

_____

_____

_____

_____

_____

_____

_____

_____

_____

_____

We're so excited you are going to join us on this journey and we hope you enjoy slaying in your own lane.

Ready? Let's begin!

Black British women are well past making waves – we're currently creating something of a tsunami. From authors to politicians, to entrepreneurs to artists, black women in the UK continue to thrive against all odds and well outside of the world's expectations. Women who look like us, grew up in similar places to us, talk like us, are shaping almost every societal sector, from the bottom and, finally, from all the way up at the top.

However, we almost never hear of the persistence, perseverance and drive that foster such success. Perhaps more importantly, we rarely hear of the failures, the flops and the insecurities that black British women have managed to push through to get to where they are today. We rarely hear about black British women, full stop. And this silence can be just as damaging as the negativity of which we're so often on the receiving end. So let's start by taking a good look at ourselves.

THE STATS

Black children are almost four times more likely to be suspended from school than white children.

Young black British people are less likely to attend the UK's most selective universities.

Black people are the most likely to suffer from blood-related diseases such as sickle cell, diabetes and hypertension.

15

Black women are more likely to use cosmetics that contain potentially harmful ingredients than other demographics.

Black people are three times more likely than white people to be admitted to hospital for mental health problems, and more likely to be detained under the Mental Health Act

Black women in the UK spend six times more than white women on hair products

Black girls are more likely to read than any other ethnic group in the UK.

Female students of mixed ethnicity and Black Caribbean origin are more likely to study STEM A-levels than white female students.

Young black British people are more likely to go to university than their white British peers.

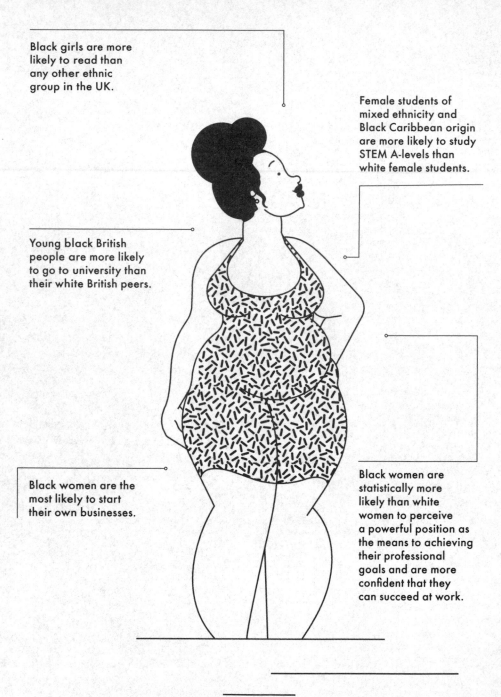

Black women are the most likely to start their own businesses.

Black women are statistically more likely than white women to perceive a powerful position as the means to achieving their professional goals and are more confident that they can succeed at work.

Before you learn how to *Slay In Your Lane*, you have to understand what slaying in your lane means. The phrase was inspired by the patron saint of black girl magic, Solange Knowles. About a week and a half after we came up with the idea of writing a book together, Liz texted Yomi a picture of Solange at Fashion Week, wearing a big red fur, with even bigger hair and killer heels. Liz captioned it in capitals with '*Slay In Your Lane*'. Yomi called her immediately and said, 'That's the name of our book.'

The photograph of Solange was taken in 2015, a year before her seminal album A Seat at the Table would be released, and at that time Solange was trying to carve out her own lane and her unique identity, away from being known as simply 'Beyoncé's younger sister'. Many of us, as black women, are trying to do the same thing – carve out a role for ourselves outside of the expectations of our families, our employers, our teachers, our friends, the world… In that picture it was clear that Solange was really coming into her own – as we hope you will too!

When we interviewed the 39 trailblazers for *Slay In Your Lane*, we asked them what slaying in your lane meant to them. Although the answers varied, the general conclusion was the same: being the best version of yourself you can. We have our own *Slay In Your Lane* definition:

STAY IN YOUR LANE:
To keep your head down,
and not get 'above your station'.

SLAY:
To excel beyond measure;
to totally 'kill it'.

SLAY IN YOUR LANE:
To flourish regardless of
perceived limitations and to
create your own version of success.

What does 'Slay In Your Lane' mean to you? Write your definition below:

_____

_____

_____

_____

_____

_____

_____

_____

_____

_____

'Sometimes, I feel discriminated against, but it does not make me angry. It merely astonishes me. How can any deny themselves the pleasure of my company? It's beyond me.'

Zora Neale Hurston

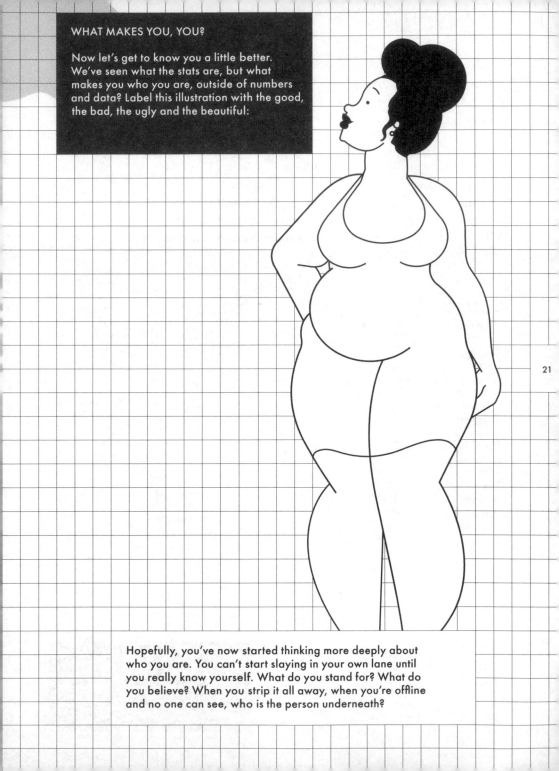

WHAT MAKES YOU, YOU?

Now let's get to know you a little better. We've seen what the stats are, but what makes you who you are, outside of numbers and data? Label this illustration with the good, the bad, the ugly and the beautiful:

Hopefully, you've now started thinking more deeply about who you are. You can't start slaying in your own lane until you really know yourself. What do you stand for? What do you believe? When you strip it all away, when you're offline and no one can see, who is the person underneath?

DESIGN YOUR OWN COAT OF ARMS

Imagine you were the ruler of your own country. What values are most important to you that you would want to instil in your citizens? Choose three or four of them from this list and add them to the coat of arms below:

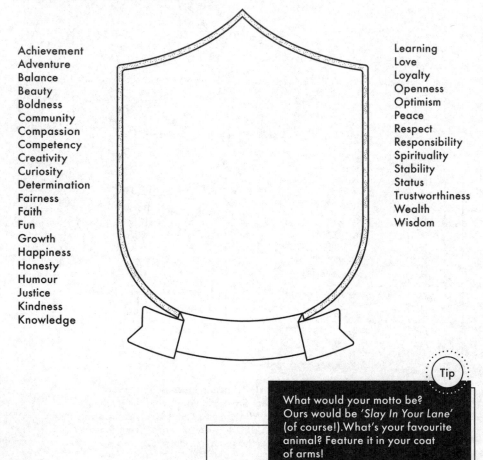

Achievement
Adventure
Balance
Beauty
Boldness
Community
Compassion
Competency
Creativity
Curiosity
Determination
Fairness
Faith
Fun
Growth
Happiness
Honesty
Humour
Justice
Kindness
Knowledge

Learning
Love
Loyalty
Openness
Optimism
Peace
Respect
Responsibility
Spirituality
Stability
Status
Trustworthiness
Wealth
Wisdom

Tip

What would your motto be? Ours would be 'Slay In Your Lane' (of course!). What's your favourite animal? Feature it in your coat of arms!

'So few young black women have role models outside of their immediate family and friends to help them navigate the inevitable hurdles that do exist. To give them valuable advice, encouragement, and support. I firmly believe that you need to see it to be it.'
Karen Blackett

According to a BBC Newsround study in 2014, about one in five black children believe their skin colour could damage their job prospects. One child told BBC Newsround's reporter, 'This generation is still being judged and stereotyped, so it's going to be difficult for us to do what we want to do when we're older.'

One of the things we hoped to achieve with *Slay In Your Lane* is to show young black girls that there is no limit to the roles they can carve out for themselves. The women interviewed in our book include actors, chief executives, sportswomen, politicians, singers, scientists, entrepreneurs and authors. As black women we tend only to be shown a narrow range of possibilities for ourselves, and we are bombarded with the idea that there are only certain roles for certain people. But increasingly there are more and more role models out there who can inspire you to realise your potential and follow your dreams. There is a saying: 'It takes a village to raise a child.' There are so many amazing black British women who have come before us and who are slaying in their proverbial lanes. We need to remind ourselves to revel in the achievements of those who ran so we could fly, as well as to encourage those who are just about to take flight. Here are just a few of these women:

Dr. Anne-Marie Imafidon

Aged 11, Anne-Marie was the youngest girl ever to pass A-level computing, and she was just 20 years old when she received her Master's Degree in Mathematics and Computer Science from the University of Oxford. She held positions at Goldman Sachs, Hewlett-Packard and Deutsche Bank and received several honorary doctorates. She went on to co-found the *STEMettes*, an award-winning social initiative dedicated to inspiring and promoting the next generation of young women in the STEM sectors.

Malorie Blackman

Malorie held the position of Children's Laureate from 2013 to 2015. She is best known for her critically acclaimed and commercially successful *Noughts and Crosses* series, which uses the setting of a fictional dystopia to explore racism and has been adapted for both stage and television. In 2018, she became the first black writer to pen an episode for the *Dr Who* television series.

Sharmadean Reid

Sharmadean started *WAH* as a hip-hop magazine for girls in 2006 while she was still at university. She then founded *WAH Nails* as a side project in 2009. She went on to deliver global pop-up nail salons for hundreds of brands and create a product line with Boots. In 2016 she opened a salon in Soho, London, showcasing a Virtual Reality Nail Design app. She went on to found Beautystack, a new social network-style marketplace for beauty professionals, and raised £4 million in funding.

Vanessa Kingori

Vanessa was a publisher at GQ *Style* UK and Associate Publisher of Fashion for *British* GQ at Condé Nast from 2009 to 2017. Vanessa became the first female publisher of *British* GQ and the first black publisher at *Condé Nast UK*. Before breaking the mould at Condé Nast, she also held leadership positions at UK publications *Esquire* and *Evening Standard's ES Magazine*. In 2017, she was officially named the new Publishing Director of *British Vogue*.

As a child who were your role models? Liz really admired the TV presenter and campaigner June Sarpong and Yomi's role model was author Malorie Blackman.

Three of my role models were:

_____

_____

_____

What about them inspired you?

_____

_____

_____

Now think about three black women you admire today, and write down three reasons why you admire each of them.

_____

_____

_____

_____

_____

_____

_____

_____

_____

_____

'If you don't like something, change it. If you can't change it, change your attitude.'
Maya Angelou

Now take a moment to celebrate yourself. What are the things you are good at? It seems like a simple enough question, but as we will see in the next chapter, many of us are often so bogged down by the expectations of everyone else, that we can lose sight of our own achievements and passions. Ask yourself, what do you like doing and what are you good at doing? You can work this out by thinking about the following questions:

What were you good at as a child? As children, we tend not to overthink things and broadly do what we enjoy and what we're good at. In your childhood you will have tried many different things, and some of those things you actually did well at without putting in much effort. What were they?

_____

_____

_____

_____

_____

_____

What would your friends say? Ask the people who genuinely know and love you about what they think you're good at. Think outside of the box!

_____

_____

_____

_____

_____

What compliments do you tend to receive? Write down the three most common ones.

_____

_____

_____

Look at these closely. You may find that you are often complimented about the same thing, and it may be that you are good at it because it's something that comes naturally to you. Perhaps it's the speed at which you did something? Or your attention to detail? The depth of knowledge you displayed?

Once you understand what your strengths are you can begin to work out how to play to them, which will in turn help you to *Slay In Your Lane*.

IMPOSTER SYNDROME

'I really don't mind failing because I think I learn a lot from my mistakes and my failures, but for me, the worst thing would be to be on my deathbed and to think, "I wish I had tried and I wish I'd had the guts to try, and it was the fear holding me back and I should never have let it do that." And that would be worse.'
Malorie Blackman

In *Slay In Your Lane*, Malorie Blackman talks about the experience of feeling like an imposter at the Black Powerlist dinner when she was on a table with other people who had achieved great things. She started wondering, 'Why am I here?' But then she reminded herself, 'No, you've been invited! You have a right to be here just as much as anybody else.' She drew on her self-belief to combat imposter syndrome.

The only person who can block you from fulfilling your ambitions is yourself. When people say, 'Can you do this?' or, 'Could you do that?' it's easy to think, 'Oh, I'm not sure that's for me,' or, 'I can't do that.' But you don't want your future self to look back and think, 'Oh, I should have done that.'

Understanding that you have a right to be in the room, a contribution to make, value to add, is key in overcoming imposter syndrome. One of the ways we deal with imposter syndrome is by writing down a list of the things we're most proud of. Sometimes it's so easy to forget all the amazing things you've achieved, because you've moved on to the next thing in your life.

Write down ten things you are most proud of (use your CV or ask your closest friends and family, if you get stuck).

_____

_____

_____

_____

_____

_____

_____

_____

_____

_____

See: you're incredible!

What's stopping you from grabbing your future with both hands? Now let's take a look at what you can do in order to get there.

'Even today when I get into a taxi and someone says "What do you do?" and I say "I'm a space scientist," they do a double take. I'm a woman and I'm black. "How come you're a space scientist? That doesn't add up."'

Dr Maggie Aderin-Pocock

We can all remember what it felt like to be a little kid, full of hopes, dreams and ambitions about the jobs we were going to have and the life we wanted to live. However, as the years pass, many different factors can often impede those ambitions and set limitations before we have time to really know what it is we want to do.

When Liz was at school, as the time came for her to start making decisions about her future, she often found herself in a no-man's land, caught between her parents' very high expectations and the lower expectations of some of her teachers – in addition to all the usual pressures of simply being a teenager.

In *Slay In Your Lane*, Dr Maggie Aderin-Pocock talks candidly about the day she realised her potential, and her outlook changed for the better. For a long time as a child, she doubted her ability, because she internalised a lot of the negative labels. However, things turned around at one specific moment for her, when she put her hand up to answer a question in class. For a moment she hesitated, and almost put her hand back down, because she thought her answer couldn't be correct. But then she decided to step outside of her comfort zone and give it a go and she got it right.

What was the most encouraging thing a teacher or your parent said to you as a child?

_____

_____

_____

What was the least encouraging?

_____

_____

_____

If you could say three encouraging things to your younger self, what would they be?

_____

_____

_____

We all know how it feels to be labelled negatively and how easy it is to start thinking those labels are true. However, if you can trust in yourself and be confident that who you are is what makes you special, then you can rip up those labels and start writing your own story.

'For me, it started with building up my confidence and self-belief, and it also meant I had to shut out the voices, inside and out, that would tell me I wasn't good enough and shouldn't be there and that I had to work harder.'
Liz

What attributes would your younger self admire about you now?

_____

_____

_____

What did you believe as a child that you know is no longer true, but which might still be holding you back? Write it down – and then scribble it out!

_____

_____

_____

_____

STEPPING OUT OF YOUR COMFORT ZONE AND DISCOVERING YOUR POTENTIAL

'It's this idea that you have to be twice as good to get half of what they have. Until girls don't have that feeling, we will have not done our jobs.'
Kerry Washington

How much of our true potential is buried under other people's expectations, our fears, our unwillingness to step outside our comfort zones?

Sometimes as black women, when we're trying 'twice as hard' and only seeming to get half as much back, it can feel easier to keep our heads down and not take too many risks.

Growing up, Liz's intense fear of failure led her to avoid trying to do new things. She eventually realised that part of believing in yourself means not worrying too much about failure or about getting things wrong. Every time she stepped out of her comfort zone and attempted something new, she was able to gain self-belief and uncover hidden talents.

Write down three of your greatest fears:

I am afraid that: _____

I am afraid that: _____

I am afraid that: _____

Pick one. Is this fear holding you back from living the life you want to live? Think about how this fear has impacted negatively in your life. Now let's reframe that fear! It's okay to have fears, you can use this fear as fuel to drive you.

Do you think it's possible to change your relationship with this fear? ☐ Yes   ☐ No

Is this a realistic or unrealistic fear?   ☐ Yes   ☐ No

Unrealistic » See, Go for it! Don't let it win or hold you back from being the best you!

Realistic » Be realistic: could this really happen, are you really sure?   ☐ Yes   ☐ No

What could be the worst thing that could happen?

_____

_____

_____

How bad would that really be?

If you've had bad experiences with this fear in the past, then it's time to think differently about it in order to prepare yourself for the next time you feel it. You will need to face the fear head on. It usually helps when you are open about your fears, so try speaking to someone else about them. Remember, your fears are likely to be exaggerated and sometimes you just need to look at them from a different perspective.

For example, try and see it as a learning experience. Liz used to have a fear of public speaking and of giving presentations to large groups of people. But after she confronted the fear head on and realised she was putting too much pressure on herself, she decided that she didn't have to be perfect.

She also started to build up her confidence by practising what she was going to say and by doing warm-up exercises. Before long, her fear had turned into nervous excitement, and she now says to herself, 'It's okay to be nervous, I can still do this. The fear won't kill me; it is simply an uncomfortable feeling and it will pass. I want to get better at public speaking so I will try.'

Say this out loud:

'I am going to be okay, no matter what happens. I will confront this feeling of fear and learn to manage it until it becomes no longer a fear of mine.'

The sky's the limit on the things you can do in life – but you've got to actually know what the opportunities are before you can work out some goals for yourself. To do this you're going to need to step outside your comfort zone, and get used to feeling a little uncomfortable...

New experiences can be unsettling at first, but there's nothing like the satisfaction of doing something you didn't think you could do. Always be on the lookout for ways to stretch yourself, both big and small.

In an ideal world, what would you attempt if you knew you could not fail?

_____

_____

_____

We all have to start somewhere. What are three small steps outside your comfort zone you could take today? It might be introducing yourself to a colleague, taking a different route home, or even simply ordering a different kind of drink in a café. Try it...you never know where those small steps might lead.

Seeing it to believe it doesn't just apply to role models. Sometimes you need to see it even more literally. A vision board is a collage that allows you to display and visualise your goals and future plans. You can use it as a daily inspiration and a reminder of what it is you want to achieve and why.

Decorate the vision board below with what you want to achieve this week, month, year and in your lifetime. Think big, but think small too...achievements come in all shapes and sizes!

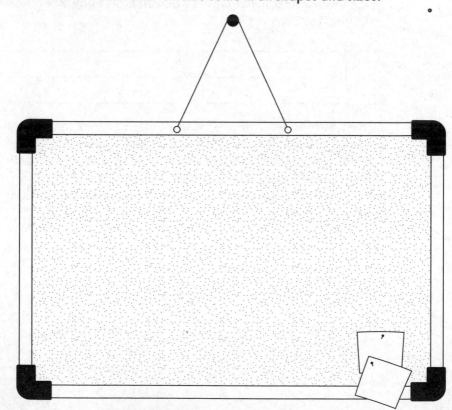

While it is important to focus on your goals and how to grow as a person, it is also helpful to look at what might be holding you back. In the spaces below, fill out six things you would like to start doing more, and six things you want to start trying to do less. For instance, you could 'do' more reading, and 'do not' waste money on junk food:

To do list

_____

_____

_____

_____

_____

To do _not_ list

_____

_____

_____

_____

_____

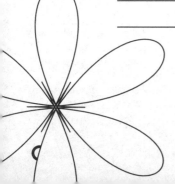

There is a famous saying by the poet John Dryden: 'First we make our habits, then our habits make us.' It's useful to track our habits, both good and bad. A habit tracker can help us to stay on track to meet goals or keep us aware of when we lapse back into bad habits. Instead of guessing how much time we spend doing a particular thing, a habit tracker accurately tracks this for us.

Fill out the habits you want to keep an eye on over the month in the two habit trackers below. Yomi has a bad habit of being late and Elizabeth has a bad habit of forgetting breakfast. If you have a habit of sleeping in, colour in every day that you did this. Or if it's something you do several times a day, like biting your nails, or interrupting people when they're talking, colour in for every time you catch yourself doing it that day.

My bad habits:	1	2	3	4	5	6	7	8	9	10	11	12	13	14	15	16	17	18	19	20	21	22	23	24	25	26	27	28	29	30

My good habits!	1	2	3	4	5	6	7	8	9	10	11	12	13	14	15	16	17	18	19	20	21	22	23	24	25	26	27	28	29	30

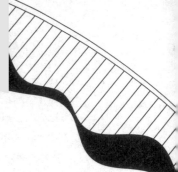

DECISIONS, DECISIONS

It's great that you have been thinking about all these plans, goals and ideas – but it can be a struggle to actually implement them. Sometimes, we can think ourselves out of action. Have you ever been faced with choices that you overthink to the point of not doing them at all? We call this to-ing and fro-ing regarding a decision so much that you never make it **analysis paralysis**. Whether it's applying for that job, starting that podcast, asking someone out or simply deciding what pair of shoes to buy, the outcome of analysis paralysis is the same: nothing.

You know you're suffering from analysis paralysis when you:
- overcomplicate even the most simple decision
- are overwhelmed by the amount of information available to you
- are overwhelmed by the number of options available to you...
- ...as well as the number of potential outcomes
- are having to make too many decisions at once
- feel like you must make the 'perfect' choice
- feel afraid making a wrong move, so you refuse to make one altogether

You shouldn't worry – being an overthinker isn't the end of the world. Smart people do a lot of thinking in order not to make rash decisions, so this can often be a good thing. But if we don't ever take action, we cannot improve our lives.

So how do we move on?

- Prioritise: what decisions need to be made immediately? What can you postpone? Focus on the ones you need to make now and save the rest for later.
- Have some perspective: not all decisions are created equal! Whilst buying a new deep conditioner is probably a low-level choice, deciding whether you want to have children is up there on the top tier. Treat them accordingly.
- Forget perfection: it doesn't really exist anyway. Done is better than perfect!
- Set a deadline: give yourself a set amount of time to reach a conclusion, and tell your friends to hold you accountable if you don't.
- Start small: pick a small part of your project that you can start. When you complete a step, treat yourself!
- Start early: most people are better at making decisions early in the day, before their mental energy and willpower have been drained by the day's choices.
- Scale back: why do some entrepreneurs like Steve Jobs wear the same clothes every day? One less decision!
- Work out what you want: before starting any research, think about what it is you really want from this choice. Once you know, it is easier to focus.
- Get another opinion: including others in the decision-making process is often incredibly helpful. It can be difficult for us to get some perspective when we are in the midst of a big decision. Talking it over with someone else helps us to clarify our own thoughts as well as providing us with a different point of view.

Now, write down three small things you have wanted to do and have had analysis paralysis over, then try using the tools above to help you complete them within a set time frame (e.g. a month):

_____time frame:_____

_____time frame:_____

_____time frame:_____

'Did the student who the teacher gave an A to have two heads?'

Analysis paralysis can be just one of the things that stop us getting things done. What else do you think might be stopping you from being the best version of you? Label some suggestions on this image:

'Work twice as hard to be considered half as good' is a saying that many black women grow up with. But it is only as we to start to experience more of the world that it really can start to hit home.

List three times in your life where you feel you've had to work twice as hard:

_____

_____

_____

If there's anyone who embodies the twice-as-hard mentality, it is Serena Williams.

Navigating and dominating the whitest-of-white sports, she rose above racism and sexism to win 23 Grand Slams. She isn't just a great female athlete or even the best black athlete: she is undisputedly one of the greatest athletes ever, a shining example of black excellence.

Serena's story gives many of us the confidence to believe that we too can achieve great things if we work twice as hard. But it's also true that this can put an unnecessary level of pressure on us. It can leave us feeling twice as self-conscious and half as confident. And this is damaging to our self-esteem.

Some days it would be good to be okay with being mediocre too, and not always have to, exhaustingly, go above and beyond to be seen as just as good.

Although there is no silver bullet that magically solves the challenges we will encounter as black women, what we do know is that we shouldn't constantly have to reach a bar of excellence that we didn't create: a bar that is built by the expectations of other people, family included.

We have to learn that when we push ourselves to be the best we can be, that should be enough. We have to create our own lane, our own version of success and our own version of good.

Our idea of success should not just be linked to external

measurements but also to how we feel inside when we are achieving these markers of 'excellence'. Having a strong sense of identity is central to this. It should be about knowing at all times what you are bringing to the table, and, just like Serena, not apologising for your femaleness and blackness. So when you encounter challenges in your life you should always remember to chase your version of good, not one that is tied to white privilege and that leaves you feeling inadequate when you've not hit the target of what it is to be both black and 'excellent'.

Write down three things you are going to stop apologising for:

_____

_____

_____

Always remember that the quest for excellence is a marathon and not a sprint. It is measured over years, not fleeting moments, over failures and missteps and, of course, what we know will be your many successes.

The truth is, it doesn't matter how you get there, or even when, as long as you do in the end. It's important to remember everyone's journey is different.

What does black excellence mean to you? Write your own definition of success below.

It's important to remember that just as everyone's journey is different, everyone, without exception, will encounter failure along the way. And this failure is as important to their success as every one of their apparent triumphs. In fact, it's a necessary part of learning how to succeed. We often learn more from our failures than our successes. When Liz failed some of her exams in her first year at university, it was the wake-up call she needed to take charge of her studies, and when Yomi applied for jobs that she didn't get, in the long run this turned out to be a blessing in disguise.

When did you last fail? What did it teach you about yourself?

I failed at: _____

It taught me _____ and _____

Use this lemon to write down some of the things you thought success was when you were growing up.

49

Now use this glass of pink lemonade to write down the things that success means to you now:

The road to slaying in your own lane and defining your version of success is a challenging yet rewarding one. There is no blueprint for the journey, but as the great Maya Angelou once said, 'Success is liking yourself, liking what you do, and liking how you do it.' As black women we understand this journey more than most, and our continued motivation and our ambition for the future is testament to that.

'And anything I have accomplished, I did so not in spite of being a black woman, but because I am a black woman.'
Gabrielle Union

'Don't think of higher education as simply the next step after A-levels, think of higher education as a pathway into a career.'

Sharmaine Lovegrove

Getting a place at university is a massive achievement. But many students choose to apply because they feel they have to, or because they believe that, if they don't, they will have in some way failed. This means that many end up on campuses they aren't quite suited to, studying subjects for the sake of it.

In our book, we spoke to food entrepreneur Alexis Oladipo who told us she would have done things differently if she'd had the chance. She would have explored other options, found more work experience and worked out what she really wanted to do before heading off to university. Instead, after graduating with a grade she wasn't happy with, she decided to return to uni a few years later to do her Master's and is now achieving exactly what she had hoped to first time around.

'It wasn't until my mid-twenties that I realised what I was really passionate about, and it makes sense that I'm excelling in it because it's what I want to do. I feel like people should just take their time, they shouldn't feel pressured by society or their parents. Take your time and really explore what it is you want to do. University is always going to be there, it doesn't have to be done when you're 18 fresh out of college, when you have no idea what life is. The world has told you, you go to college and then you go to university and then you get a lotta debt – at least get into debt for something that you're going to use!'

So before deciding to go to university, you should be a hundred per cent sure about whether you need to go right now or rather, if you need to go at all:

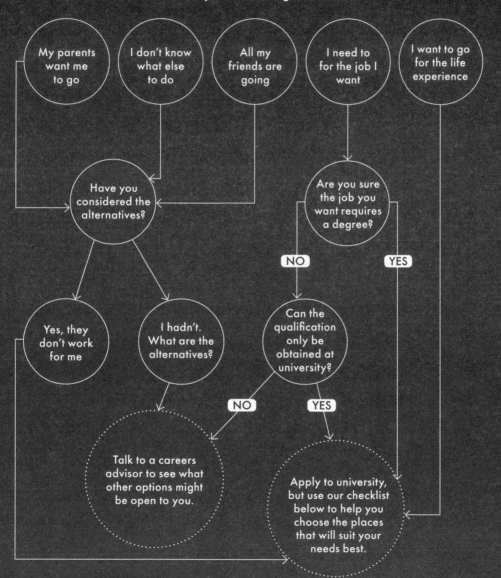

My parents want me to go

I don't know what else to do

All my friends are going

I need to for the job I want

I want to go for the life experience

Have you considered the alternatives?

Are you sure the job you want requires a degree?

NO

YES

Yes, they don't work for me

I hadn't. What are the alternatives?

Can the qualification only be obtained at university?

NO

YES

Talk to a careers advisor to see what other options might be open to you.

Apply to university, but use our checklist below to help you choose the places that will suit your needs best.

53

If you've decided to go to university, that's great. And if you haven't, that's also good – whatever works for you and your future.

Now, it's important to make sure you go to the right university for you. When doing your research into the various institutions, use the following checklist for guidance:

1. What can your potential uni offer in the way of courses and facilities? Are you happy with what's available?

2. Have you looked at all the degrees that are on offer? Is your choice best suited to your future career?

3. Have you researched what kind of a reputation your uni has for the course you are doing? What kind of results are students getting? Might there be other universities that have a better reputation for your course?

4. What is the vibe/culture of the university (you should be able to find this out by doing some online research/ reading student newspapers/blogs, etc.)? Will it suit you?

5. Are you happy with living in the city/area where it is located?

6. Have you explored all options in terms of universities? Have you kept an open mind?

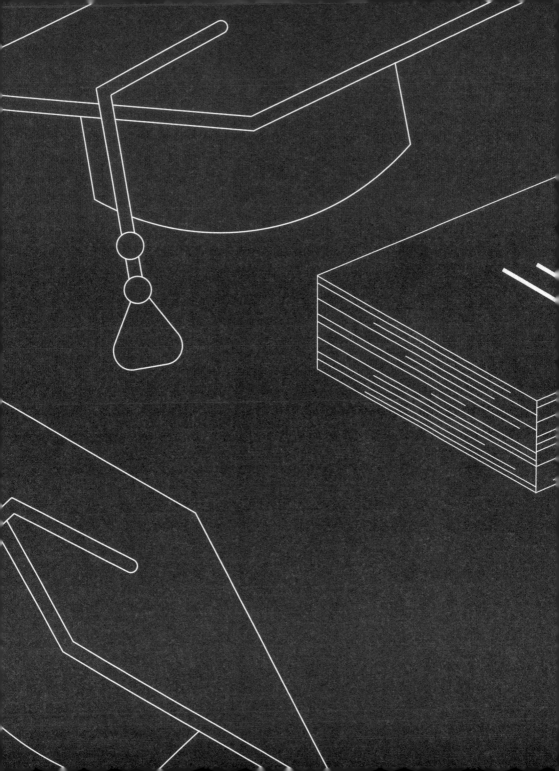

WILL I FIT IN?

University was one of the greatest times of our lives, but it wasn't without its challenges. For many students, university is often the first time they will come across individuals from different backgrounds to their own. For some black students, it can be the first time they have lived in a predominantly white area. It's not unusual for black university students to experience feelings of exclusion.

Friends matter at university and they can provide a great support network when things get difficult – it's where we met and if we hadn't this book wouldn't exist! For many students, societies can quickly become a second home and an outlet for hobbies old and new. For black students in particular, societies such as the ACS (African-Caribbean Society) can be a way of ensuring you meet other students from similar backgrounds who may be experiencing similar things.

1. Write down three of your favourite hobbies

2. Write down three types of people you'd like to meet

3. Write down three qualities/skills you want to improve in

Use these lists to help you join at least three societies when you start uni.

1.

2.

3

'We question whether we belong there and whether we have the right to be there, and I think that you've got to try and flip that on its head and think, I need to rinse this place for every drop I can get out of it. I'm going to use it before it uses me. I worked that out and it really helped. I was like, you know what, whatever I can get from this place is going to give me what I need for my journey, I'm going to rinse it.'

Afua Hirsch, journalist and author

Five Black Girl Student Survival Tips:

1. Locate the shops that stock ethnic foods before getting there, via forums or on Google.

2. Try and do the same with hairdressers – look online or find a student who does hair (there is always one).

3. Stock seasonings and your family's cooking from trips home – you will miss it and will need it!

4. If your uni lacks diversity, mingle with local, more diverse students from neighbouring universities, as well as locals who aren't students – they will tell you where the clubs that play black music are.

5. If there isn't an active anti-racism society already, don't be afraid to create one! ACSs are about culture, whilst anti-racism societies are about fighting discrimination on and off campus.

**OPERATION SECURE THE BAG:
SLAY YOUR PERSONAL FINANCES**

'I felt like it was time to set up my future, so I set a goal. My goal was independence.'

Beyoncé

In *Slay In Your Lane*, Charlene White talks about buying her first house and the independence it gave her:

'I bought my house at 24, and all by myself with no help. I don't come from money or anything, so it's not like Dad could find a spare tens of thousands to give to me as a deposit! During the whole process of going through it I was completely fine, not emotional about it whatsoever, until the day that it completed and the solicitor called me to say that it was done, and I was standing in the middle of Richmond, and I burst into tears.

'I was trying to explain it to my dad, the reason why, and he was like, "I don't understand why you're getting so emotional, it's just bricks and mortar!" and I'm like, "It's about more than that, it's, it's my independence, it's the biggest thing I have ever done all by myself."'

Money matters: not only because of its functional benefits – paying bills and buying the things we need – but because the value we place on money is inseparable from the opportunity it gives us to be independent.

But let's be honest, the complexity of the financial system doesn't make things easier for us; it effectively excludes those who don't have the tools to understand it. Wherever you are in your financial journey, whether you're focused on getting out of your student debt, wanting to save for a house deposit or just a holiday, or simply want to feel more in control of your outgoings, when you take your first steps towards financial independence, it can feel overwhelming.

Everyone's circumstances are different: personal finance is exactly that – personal. However, we can all agree that money should give you choices and that real freedom comes from being able to use it to live life the way you want to. Getting closer to your finances allows you to create a life with experiences that are tailored to you. It's never too late to get started, or to get better at it.

Financial independence looks like:

_____

_____

Being empowered about my finances would make me:

_____

_____

Being in a good state with my finances would look like:

_____

_____

Over the following pages we will explore your financial mindset, helping you take control and be in the driving seat of your financial future, because there is no time like the present to come up with a plan!

Before we look at your current finances and set some goals for the future, let's think about your early money memories. Often the messages we are taught or not taught as kids (consciously or unconsciously) can have a significant impact on our financial decisions today.

Liz wasn't taught any practical money-management skills at school or at home; her understanding of money started and stopped with what it could buy you. Her first money memory is of when she was 11 and she spent her bus money on sweets, boneless wing meals for her friends and a trip to the arcade. As Liz sat anxiously at the bus stop knowing she would be in serious trouble when she finally made it home, that was the first time in her life she realised the importance of being responsible with money and the consequences of money mismanagement.

In *Slay In Your Lane*, Jamelia describes her early relationship with money in similar terms. Her introduction to it came when she signed her first record deal at the age of 15. Essentially you could say her first job was being 'Jamelia', the singer. 'One day you're in a council house and the next day they're giving you a cheque that's more than your mum's annual salary. At 15, the first thing I did, I went out and I bought trainers for my whole class at school. I didn't have any financial advice, I was a child being given stupid amounts of money.'

What is your earliest money memory?

_____

_____

_____

_____

63

What is your best experience with money?

_____

_____

_____

_____

What is your worst?

_____

_____

_____

_____

What is the best financial advice you've ever received?
Who gave it you?

_____

_____

_____

_____

How has that positively impacted your financial life?

_____

_____

_____

_____

It is very likely that your relationship with money today will
be shaped to a large extent by your finances when you were
growing up. But whether your early money memories were
good or bad, and whether what you learned from your parents
about money management was positive or negative, now is the

time you can redefine your relationship with money on your own terms. To start, let's explore your financial attitudes when it comes to how you manage and spend your money.

Describe your relationship with money in three words:

_____

_____

Finish this sentence: I wish that money was

_____

_____

_____

At some point all of us have probably experienced stress and anxiety about the state of our finances. Do you have any money fears? If so, what are they?

_____

_____

What is your ultimate weakness when it comes to spending money responsibly?

_____

_____

_____

_____

Does it take you off track from your short- and long-term financial goals?

☐ Yes ☐ No

Are you an avoider who hopes financial difficulties will magically sort themselves out?

☐ Yes ☐ No

Do you channel your stress into other things? (This could mean going to the gym more often, eating more, maybe even shopping more.)

☐ Yes ☐ No

If yes, what are those things?

_____

_____

_____

_____

_____

If you answered yes to any of the questions above, don't worry – you're not alone! But slaying at your personal finances is a big part of slaying in your lane and we're here to help.

WHAT IS YOUR MONEY STORY?

When it comes to managing your finances, do you notice that some of your friends seem to have it more together than others? Perhaps they use financial language confidently and are knowledgeable about their financial situation. On the other hand, you might have other friends who don't understand the basics of savings accounts, how to use a credit card properly and the impact of credit scores, or even how much they have left in their bank account at the end of every month. To help you figure out what personality you are, when it comes to money, meet this squad of four friends having dinner.

1. The living in the moment and spontaneous kind. They prefer to live life to the fullest through experiences, i.e. holidaying and going out. They don't have a long-term financial plan because they haven't even thought about it. 'Live for today, worry about it tomorrow' and 'Put it on the credit card,' they say regularly. They order champagne by the glass and have three glasses and the steak.

2. A reforming shopaholic, they make impulse purchases led by their heart, and instantly regret it. They two-step around their finances, generally pay their bills on time, and have a few loans they are paying off due to bad decisions in the past. They constantly procrastinate when it comes to financial tasks. They have two cocktails and choose the chicken.

3. Financially comfortable and optimistic about their financial affairs. They are ambitious, driven to earn

more, have financial goals, and are confident about achieving them. No debt apart from student loans. They enjoy the finer things in life not because they have lots of money but because they are currently managing their money very well and make trade-offs (see page 75). They have a glass of wine and the fish.

4. The prudent saver. They've been saving for a rainy day since you've met them, they don't invest their money because they are risk-averse. They actively manage their finances, obsess over their bank balances and avoid borrowing money at all costs. They live well within their means, almost too much at times. You worry it stops them enjoying life. Friends say they need to live a little. They have tap water and the chicken.

After reflecting on this range of different money behaviours, which money personality best describes you? You might be a mixture of two!

I am a _____

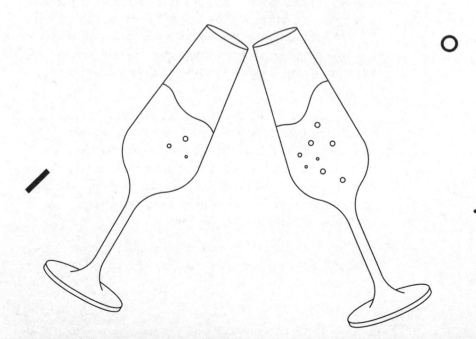

The Fidelity Investments' Money FIT Women Study in 2015 found that eight in ten women would refrain from discussing money with family and friends because they felt too uncomfortable about it or thought that it was too personal.

Having spoken to many of our friends, we've all had similar experiences: we were taught that talking about money is somehow uncouth, unladylike and bad-mannered. But it's not and we have to break the taboo!

The awkward truth is, money is often linked to status, and status is linked to power. If you don't have a lot of the former, talking about it can make people feel like they're powerless, which results in a dearth of meaningful conversations around it. But money is a form of power, and full equality for women means financial equality.

There's power in having open conversations about money. Try it and see! If possible, open up to your close friends – you could ask them which one of the money personalities they think they are in the list above – and encourage them to talk about how they feel about money.

How did it feel?

_____

_____

_____

_____

_____

They say it's often an unexpected situation that inspires us to really take a closer look at our finances. But we say it's better not to wait for unexpected and instead you should take that closer look now.

Spend a few minutes looking at your latest bank statements or your current money app with your accounts. Is there a recurring feeling that comes to mind?

Anger? Anxiety? Panic? Depression? Shame? Happiness? Contentment? Indifference?

Use this space to write about how your bank statements make you feel:

_____

_____

If those feelings are negative, how would you like to feel about your money instead?

_____

_____

_____

Now use one of your bank statements to fill out this monthly expenses table.

ITEMS	BUDGET	ACTUAL AMOUNT	DIFFERENCE	MY NOTES
Income				
Outgoing				
Total				

Tip

If you separate your outgoings into different categories, this will help you see where you might be able to cut down unnecessary expenditure effectively. It will also help you when you come to think about possible trade-offs (see page 75).

After filling out this table, you could try the popular Kakeibo method of budgeting. It's a great way to reflect and think mindfully about your money.

How much money do you have available?

_____

_____

How much would you like to save?

_____

_____

How much are you spending?

_____

_____

_____

How can you improve?

_____

_____

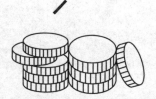

BUDGET. BUDGET. BUDGET.

It goes without saying that you should be spending less than you earn. Some people use the 50–20–30 rule to help them stick to this:

- 50 per cent of what you earn goes to living expenses and essentials; for example, rent, utilities, groceries and travel costs for getting to work.
- 20 per cent goes to financial goals, your savings, investments, and debt-reduction payments.
- 30 per cent is for flexible spending: eating out, make-up, going out, cinema.

On the next page, fill out three money habits you would like to start doing more, and three things you want to start trying to do less.

Tip

Consider managing your finances via the new range of personal budgeting apps. They are a great way to keep track of your spending: they show you how much you spend on little things, such as coffee, and text you when you're closing in on your budget. They can even save money on your behalf. You can get a text message at the start of every week about how much money you have in your current accounts; it forces you to understand your spending habits – for better or for worse.

Tip

Cancel memberships and subscriptions that you are not using; it's the easiest way to cut your outgoings.

73

Bad money habits you want to leave behind

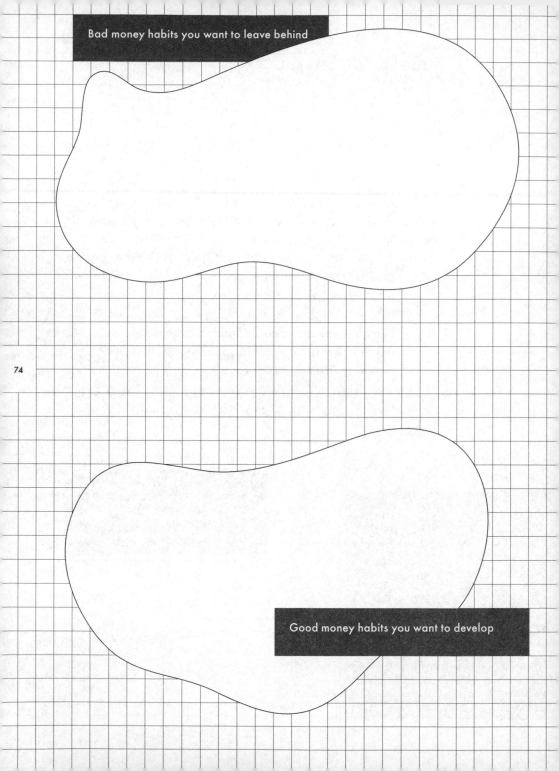

Good money habits you want to develop

'And I had to decide then, "Do I rent with some of my friends? And be in the thick of it and just enjoy this moment? Or do I trade it off?" And I decided to trade it off.'
Vanessa Kingori

Savings are vital, providing a safety net against dips in income and unplanned situations. Even in relatively small amounts, savings can help people avoid debt or severe hardship.

As a result of the ethnic minority pay gap, black women are less likely to have the opportunity to build up significant savings for a rainy day. And living in England, if there's one thing we understand, it's that when it rains, boy can it pour. We all know that life doesn't always go to plan, but you're more financially vulnerable to emergencies if you have found it difficult to save.

Many do not have the luxury of building up an emergency fund, or what writer Paulette Perhach calls a 'fuck-off fund', that gives you the freedom to live the life you want, or just to fuck off from a toxic relationship, job or household situation.

But with a bit of thought and some planning – and if we're prepared to give certain things up for the moment, in order to reap the benefit later – we can all be better prepared for that rainy day.

In the last section, we looked at your outgoings. Now you can use that information to create a budget that compares your expenses to your income, so you can then establish 'SMART' ('specific, measurable, ambitious, relevant and time-sensitive') long-term financial goals.

These goals are unique to everyone and they could be a house deposit, a holiday or a car, or simply getting out of your overdraft.

WHAT ARE YOU SAVING FOR?

MY SHORT-TERM FINANCIAL GOALS	APPROXIMATE COST

MY LONG-TERM FINANCIAL GOALS	APPROXIMATE COST
TOTAL	

Now prioritise them, ordering them by number. Don't think about how you will pay for them right now, focus on the goals and their approximate cost. Now you have your goals, you can think about what choices you can make to bring your outgoings down and add to your savings so that you can reach those goals as quickly as possible.

Vanessa Kingori, publisher at *British Vogue*, says:

'It's understanding that every single thing in life is a trade-off. If you want the small thing, and you're like, "I just want it," you have to have in your mind that at the time you're getting the small thing, this is going to mean that it's going to take you longer to get that other thing. It's also my time, which is hands-down, I think, our most valuable, my most valuable, asset now.

'When I was saving to buy my current property, I just was living slightly out, and all of my friends were moving to East London. I had quite a good set-up, in that I was paying really low rent where I was and it worked with getting to work. And it was a really defining moment for me, I wanted to be there on the Friday night with everyone. But I also wanted to own my own property, and I wanted to not be pouring my money away in rent. And I had to decide then, "Do I rent with some of my friends? And be in the thick of it and just enjoy this

Tip

You can find many different budgeting tools and templates online – we recommend https://www.moneyadviceservice.org.uk/en/tools/budget-planner – and you can take the information from your expenses table above, and the goals table below, to fill in your own personal budget.

moment? Or do I trade it off?" And I decided to trade it off and stay in West London. Now both had value to them, it's just what was important for me. But you have to know what you're trading at the time and you have to think that through. That's literally how I think about everything – from career opportunities, to time, to purchases, to extra jobs and work that I take on. In a way, everybody is doing this, they just don't always know that they are.'

What trade-offs can you make to get you to your savings and investment goals quicker?

_____

_____

_____

Use this space to brainstorm different ways you could make small but effective changes to your daily habits to save money:

_____

_____

_____

_____

_____

_____

_____

IS YOUR MONEY WORKING FOR YOU OR FOR EVERYONE ELSE?§

Trade-offs are a fantastic way of helping you save, but they aren't always easy to do. A recent study in a new report from Credit Karma revealed that nearly 40 per cent of Millennials have gone into debt just to keep up with their friends' lifestyles.

Debt is a very scary thing, and it is something that singer VV Brown experienced when she was 21: 'I got signed to Universal at 18 and moved to LA. I made an album, bought a house, lived like a rock star, got ill-advised and lost everything. I got shelved and at 21 I was in debt to over £100,000. It was one of the worst times in my life. I still look back on it and I can't believe that I got through it.

79

'When I paid it back and then started to make money again, there were so many things I learned – from opening up a tax account specifically for your tax so you're always organised financially; get yourself the right accountant; open up several accounts and distribute your money across different accounts; categorise your accounts specifically. Now I have an account for my personal life, which is where I pay myself a salary, I have a limited company, but I also have separate accounts for things like childcare, car and cleaner.'

Even when you are making money and things start looking up financially, it can be easy to fall into the trap of overspending and living beyond your means. It is all too easy to succumb to peer pressure and the fear of missing out, particularly in these times, when social media comparisons can be just a click and a like away. Now it only takes an hour of perusing your favourite apps to believe you know what you need to own in order to keep up with the world. The truth is, of course, that social media is just a highlights reel, a curated snapshot of people's lives, and we have to remember that it deliberately captures only the most glamorous aspects of those lives.

Have you ever found yourself trying to influence other people's opinions of your financial status, either by impressing them or downplaying how much you have?

Melanie Eusebe, the co-founder of the BBB Awards (Black British Business Awards), understands all too well the burdens of consumerism fuelled by social media. In Slay In Your Lane she explains:
'You have all these things, and then you don't use them or you don't need them. When you start actually budgeting, [you realise] how much money you spent on things that you no longer use or want or desire.
'I wish I had known a bit more about myself in terms of what made me really, really happy, so I could invest in it. And what would've made me really happy is having my own business and having freedom to do whatever I wanted on projects and stuff – not work for a little bit, to travel for a little bit – rather than be beholden to bills. I've learned that the things I purchase don't make me happy.'

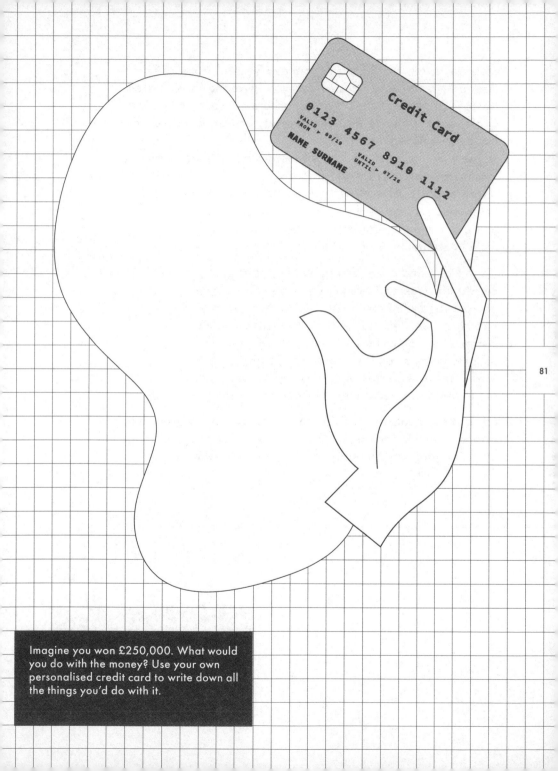

Imagine you won £250,000. What would you do with the money? Use your own personalised credit card to write down all the things you'd do with it.

Now review it. Do these things make you truly happy? Are they only temporary fixes or are you investing in your well-being? Circle the things that contribute to your well-being. Cross out the things that are unlikely to really make you happy in the long term.

There is a middle ground. Vanessa Kingori says to take a 'gains, rewards, hard work' approach.

'I was taught to, every time I was paid, have a mini celebration, because if you try to be too frugal, you get to a point where you just want to splurge, right? And then you blow it all.

'So try and find a sense of a middle, so if you're constantly thinking, "I remember when I got these earrings and what for," think: a) it gives a sense of meaning to the things that you own. And b) it feels better when you wear it, it's not just, "Oh I got that at some point, when I was splurging continuously." And it just gives a sort of quality to how you live, the experiences you have, they mean something.'

Look at the goals that you set in the 'Know your worth, then add tax' section (on page 113). When you achieve your long-term life goal, what would you like your reward to be?

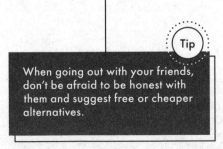

Tip

When going out with your friends, don't be afraid to be honest with them and suggest free or cheaper alternatives.

INVESTMENTS: THE FUTURE AND BEYOND

'We have to learn about stocks and shares, in the way that we know about lipstick, hair and make-up. We need to make sure we know about this stuff. It's really important, because that's what gives you independence and freedom.'
June Sarpong

The Money FIT study also found that 92 per cent of women were keen to learn about money and finances and only 7 per cent of women would currently give themselves an 'A' for their knowledge of investing.

Buying a house isn't the only form of investment opportunity out there. Studies show that, compared to white people, black people in the UK have a lower participation across the range of financial products, including ISAs, Premium Bonds and stocks and shares.

Is investing something you're interested in doing? If so, firstly, speak to someone in your bank or to a financial advisor. They can advise you on how to make the most of your money. Secondly, if you do choose to invest your money, be sure to do your research – don't commit to an investment or financial product if you don't fully understand it. Always ask questions!

What would you like your financial life to look like in ten years' time? For example, do you want to own your own home or invest in small businesses?

Your credit score plays a key role in your financial journey. It is a number that evaluates your credit-worthiness to lenders such as banks and businesses and is based on your credit history. They use credit scores to evaluate the probability that you will repay them back, thus it is a deciding factor in whether you'll be approved for a mortgage, credit card or loan. You've probably already willingly or unwillingly contributed to your credit score rating, negatively or positively. But, if you don't know it, find out.

☐ I am paying all my bills on time.

☐ I am contributing to my pension.

Most employers have a scheme that you can sign up to where they contribute to your pension plan. If in doubt, get in touch with your HR department to find out details. Why do pensions matter? You're not going to be able to work forever, so it's never too early to start planning for your retirement.

☐ I am on the right tax codes and all my tax records are up to date.

Through trade-offs and better budgeting I am building an emergency fund (three to six months of expenses).

☐ I am setting aside _____ % of my income every month.

Tip

Speak to your HR department at work or call HMRC to double check you're on the right tax code if you're not sure.

'For a long time I defined myself by what I wasn't. My life changed when I focused on what I was good at, what I liked most about myself and what made me stand out.'

Issa Rae

In today's world, it's important to build a personal brand, whether you're a graduate or a professional with years of experience, because with every person you meet, or every time someone lands on your social media page, they will be exposed to an element of who you are. And you can influence what that element will be.

People with successful brands are clear about who they are and how to play to their strengths. Karen Blackett has forged a successful career by not only being aware of and faithful to her personal brand, but also choosing to leave companies where she was not valued for who she was:

'Once you know your own personal brand and feel comfortable in your own skin, you don't have to try and morph into something else to succeed.

'When you're constantly trying to be something you're not, you're gonna be bloody unhappy. If you are in an organisation where you fear you have to morph into something else, or be something that you're not, leave.'

In an ideal world, people would give less of a shit about what you look like, listen to, speak like and eat like at work and more about, you know, your work. But for now, learning how to move between different audiences, styles and approaches when at work should also mean keeping your true self and sanity intact.

85

So, what does a personal brand even mean? You might think branding is only relevant for businesses, that it's to do with logos and company mission statements. Or you might be thinking to yourself, 'If I'm good at my job, then that should speak for itself.' Yes it should, and it does, and producing great work is one element of building a good personal brand. But a personal brand is more than that. It's also about your reputation for how you do great work. It's what people say about you when you're not in the room.

When people are considering who should lead a particular project or who to promote, being at the forefront of their minds by having a strong and consistent personal brand will propel you forwards and make you stand out in a competitive sea of professionals.

It's important to understand what a successful personal brand looks like.

1. List three people you admire most in your industry:

2. Now make a list of two things that come to mind when you think of each of them:

Our guess is that these people each have a distinctive personal brand. For example, they might have a memorable style of communication, or a distinct leadership style, or a signature phrase they often say. Bearing this in mind, can you think about what it is that feels unique to you about them? The chances are this will be at the core of their personal brand.

1.

2.

LET'S DEFINE YOUR PERSONAL BRAND

Remember, your brand is your own personal calling card – a unique promise of value and an authentic representation of you. Ultimately, to understand your brand is to understand what makes you unique and therefore what makes you stand out. The first step to building your personal brand is to perform a self-assessment.

1. How would you introduce yourself and what you do? (Write this in no more than three short sentences.)

2. You might want to have your CV at hand for this next bit. Find three words that best describe you and the impact you want to make. To help you, think about what you love doing the most and what truly excites you! But don't overthink it. For example you might want to use words like 'creative', 'enterprising', 'forward thinking', 'collaborative'. This will form the core of your brand.

3. What are your personal values? You could look back to the coat of arms you filled in at the beginning of the journal to remind you of these (page 22). These values are at the heart of how you do your work. They are your personal touch. For example, 'integrity', 'empathy' and 'community'.

4. What are you naturally good at? What do you do better than most people? Write down three things. *Hint*: this is what sets you apart from the competition and shows how you can provide value to your industry in a unique way.

1.

2.

3.

4.

5. Then think about how you can combine it all into a short sentence to communicate clearly what you stand for. For example, are you a collaborative, community-driven creative? This sentence should be simple and memorable, and it should feel inspiring to you.

Now think about the contribution you want to make. What are the skills and values you want people to associate you with? Imagine that someone you respect in your industry is emailing another person in the same industry. Person A says, 'I am working on this new project and I need someone who (what you want to be known for)'. Person B says, 'I know (insert your name) because they are the expert in (insert your area of expertise).'

It's time to validate this with feedback. Sense-check your answers with those around you. Personal brands aren't created in a vacuum. How you think you are and how others perceive you may be two opposing things. What words do others use to describe you?

Be prepared for any unexpected feedback you may receive! Sometimes our actions and behaviour don't necessarily come across to others the way we intend them to. But you may also find that you have strengths and hidden talents you're unaware of.

6. Write down their feedback here:

7. Is the person they've described the same as the person you described in your earlier sentence?

■ Yes   ■ A little   ■ No

If you ticked 'No', revisit your earlier statement and ask the person how and why they think the two differ, so you can see how you can bridge the gap.

5.

_____

_____

_____

_____

I want to be a leader in _____ and be known for_____

_____

6.

_____

_____

_____

_____

_____

_____

_____

YOUR STORY

Storytelling increases the impact of your personal brand. We all have stories that help explain how we have become the person we are, and people will always want to know your story, so that they can identify with you and what you do. These stories help reinforce your credibility.

1. Think about your life currently, about the obstacles and challenges you've faced, about your triumphs, and your successes. Write down three key events in your life that have made you who you are today.

Don't be afraid to tell these stories to other people. They are at the heart of your personal brand, and they are also likely to be inspiring to others!

2. Look back to the answer you gave at the beginning of this exercise on page 89. How would you introduce yourself now?

Is there a good story you can think of about you, which you can use as part of your brand? Perhaps something that explains why it is you do what you do. For example, you can tell people that helping the next generation is one of your personal values but it's more impactful if you tell them the story about how and why you pitched to your boss a careers and skills day for the local school.

1.

2.

PERSONAL BRAND TIPS

When people understand your personal brand, you increase your chances of connecting with others, and of finding a sponsor. As Karen Blackett explains in *Slay In Your Lane*:

> **'I think if black women are finding it difficult to get a sponsor, it's because they haven't worked out their own personal brand to have somebody be able to advocate for them. So once you've worked that out – and it takes time, it takes rewriting and rewriting, sitting there, saying it out loud, and writing it down to be able to articulate it – you've then got to stress-test it to see what somebody else thinks.'**

94

As you progress in your career, keep a balance between achieving great things and looking for opportunities to build 'brand you'. They may not be directly related to your everyday job – for example, taking on a project at work that you're passionate about that aligns with your personal brand outside of your nine-to-five, or improving your speaking skills and volunteering to take part in a panel – but by exploring those opportunities you will have the chance to further develop yourself and forge new connections.

Rome wasn't built in a day, and neither will your personal brand be. But consistency is key here, and when you're consistent in your brand you will have more opportunity to build a strong reputation and stand out in a competitive professional field – meaning you'll no longer have to chase all the opportunities, they'll start chasing you...

USE THIS BILLBOARD TO CREATE AN ADVERT FOR YOUR OWN PERSONAL BRAND!

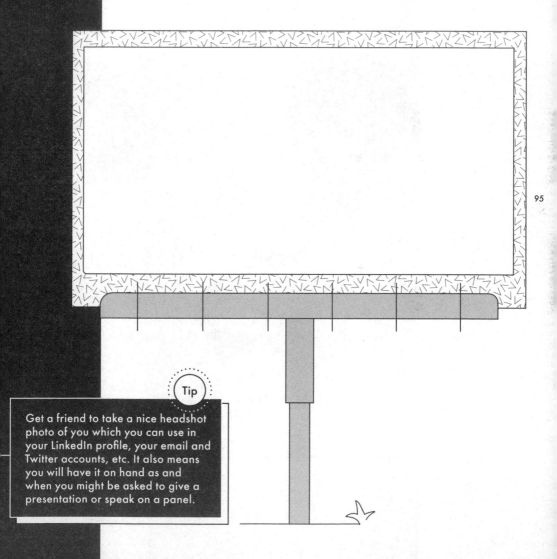

Tip

Get a friend to take a nice headshot photo of you which you can use in your LinkedIn profile, your email and Twitter accounts, etc. It also means you will have it on hand as and when you might be asked to give a presentation or speak on a panel.

'While I think all women are superheroes, we are not superhuman and we need each other's support. We need to give each other grace when we fall short – and when society sets unrealistic expectations or our workplaces have antiquated rules. We must band together and fight for what's fair.'

Serena Williams (IWD op-ed for *Fortune*)

Being black and British, people know our parents are from somewhere else before we even open our mouths. Or if not our parents, our grandparents. Or our great-grandparents. We are tattooed with our otherness. We are hyper-visible in predominantly white spaces. Yet somehow we often remain unseen, and especially unheard.

It is this frustrating paradox that fires our desire for meaningful change. But things are changing slowly and we are forcing those around us not only to see us but also to hear us by campaigning for equality in the law, in business and in wider society. With our newfound ability to speak up, we hope we can all begin to feel less apologetic about taking up space in a country that is often rigged against us.

This section is about encouraging you to be unafraid to be the person who creates that space and starts that conversation at your university, workplace or local community if it isn't already happening. We will look at how you can identify the change you may want to make and then brainstorm some ideas to get you started.

'Being a part of this re-emergence of a movement both pro-diversity and pro-woman is the best part of being a black girl. It's more than, "I stand for this because I should." I stand for this because this is part of who I am as a human being.'
Yara Shahidi

'*When they go low, we go high.*'
Michelle Obama

Chances are, as a black woman working or studying in what is likely to be a predominantly white space, you might have experienced a microaggression: i.e. someone making a comment about your hair, questioning your authority or assuming you're the spokesperson for all black people, black slang and black cultural trends.

Racism is fluid. It has changed over time, but it hasn't disappeared. Instead it has assumed a more casual, implicit form which is often more covert, indirect and ambiguous. Because of this it can be hard to identify and confront it and we often find ourselves asking, 'Am I overreacting? Did that just happen? Did they really say that?'

'*#BlackWomenAtWork are paid less, asked to do more, are constantly antagonised, and then called angry/abrasive for setting boundaries.*'
Tora Shae

Have you experienced a microaggression? Use this space to record what happened:

_____

_____

_____

_____

_____

_____

_____

_____

What thoughts were going through your mind?

_____

_____

_____

_____

_____

After it happened, how did it make you feel?

_____

_____

_____

_____

_____

Would you do anything different if it were to happen again?

_____

_____

_____

_____

_____

'I didn't learn to be quiet when I had an opinion.
The reason they knew who I was is because I TOLD
THEM.'
Ursula Burns

If we are to speak out as black women, we need to be able to
do so without fear of repercussion. Companies need to take
more seriously the duty of care they have to their employees

and to have a zero-tolerance approach to all types of racism in the workplace. How will they learn if we are unable to speak out and tell our truth? So how does one navigate these situations? How do we speak out against microaggressions without paying too high a price?

Dawn Butler, MP, told us in *Slay In Your Lane* that it depends on the circumstances:

'So you have to tailor it to whatever the situation allows, unless you want to go into full destructive mode. One of the best bits of advice I was given is to choose your battles, because when you're young you fight everything. I fought everything when I was young and that's all good, you've got the energy. When you get older you realise that you're tired and you can't always fight everything. You have to choose your battles.'

Dawn has done it in various ways.

- Disrupting – she's challenged, straight up, to their face, 'What makes you think you can address me in that manner?'
- Discreetly challenging about their racism, about their unconscious bias
- Letting the media take care of it, and have the shock factor of, yes, this is what has happened

If you find that microaggressions are a continuous problem in your workplace, book in some time with your manager. Go prepared and list the occasions, time and dates and people involved in these incidents, so you have evidence.

Depending on the situation, there's nothing wrong with disrupting and challenging microaggressions: standing firm in your convictions rather than bottling it up in an effort to rise above.

'MediaCom were actually quite good, but there's no way we would ever have had a female business director, let alone a black one.'
Unnamed white male, quoted by Karen Blackett in Slay In Your Lane, *referring to why he didn't hire her company, MediaCom*

These types of everyday microaggressions have sparked several conversations and motivated various campaigns, one of the most high-profile being the 'I, too, am Oxford' series, inspired by the 'I, too, am Harvard' initiative in America. In 2014, Oxford students organised a photoshoot consisting of portraits of BAME attendees of the university, highlighting the ignorance they came across at Oxford – and confronting it.

'I'm no longer accepting the things I cannot change...I'm changing the things I cannot accept.'
Angela Davis

It's okay to be angry. *Slay In Your Lane* itself was born out of a mix of exasperation and frustration. It was the fire that stoked our determination to write it.

Melanie Eusebe agrees: 'Anger is such a passionate, driving force, and I encourage people to acknowledge and recognise the anger. I remember a magazine interviewing me and they were saying, "Advice for young women?" and I was saying, "I want them to get angry!" Anger is a beautiful, healthy emotion that says to us, "Our boundaries have been crossed." Do not take away that anger, because there are some things that women should be angry about.

These are the injustices I am most angry about:

_____

_____

_____

_____

_____

Now it's time to educate yourself on these issues. Choose one of these injustices and think about what might be the cause of this problem you have identified. What are the consequences of this problem?

_____

_____

_____

_____

_____

_____

Can you think of any solutions to this problem?

_____

_____

_____

_____

Tip

Stay abreast with the latest developments on these issues by following the news and connecting with like-minded people on social media.

What change do you think you might be able to implement?

_____

_____

_____

_____

Would this make a lasting change in people's lives?

_____

_____

_____

_____

What is your message for change? Why should they care?

_____

_____

_____

_____

Tip

You'll need to be passionate about your cause and clear about the change you want to make.

Great, we've established your passion about the issue and your confidence in affecting change. Now let's start bringing this all to life!

105

- Use the internet to do some research into the problem you've identified. Are there people or decision-makers already doing things to help alleviate this problem? Is there an opportunity for you to join an existing campaign?
- Take the initiative and connect with others! Who else is fighting the good fight?
- Have a think about who you need to influence in order to implement change. For example, local council, decision makers, teachers, local community, the media, businesses, etc.
- If you want to raise the profile of your campaign, or change the law or policy, speaking to your local MP is a good way to get your voice heard. You can find contact details for your MP online, as well as more information about them here: www.parliament.uk/ findyourmp

Tip

Identify three things which would help achieve your objective, for example, 'I need my local MP to...'

It's time to take action. Write a list of the people you want to influence and then look up their contact details:

NAME	CONTACT DETAILS

Before contacting anyone, make sure you:
- can sum up clearly what your campaign is trying to achieve
- have evidence supporting your issue
- have thought about how your issue fits with the person's interests
- have a clear idea of why you want them to be involved
- have thought about the one action you would like them to do

Social media is a powerful tool you can use to spread awareness of your message to a large audience. For example, #BlackLivesMatter became a hashtag in the summer of 2013, after the death of Trayvon Martin, an unarmed African-American teenager. Started by three black women – Alicia Garza, Patrisse Cullors, and Opal Tometi – it has since evolved well beyond a hashtag into a real political force.

Alicia Garza, Black Lives Matter Co-Founder, says: 'Today's black power is transforming democracy – but we cannot do it alone. We need the best and the brightest thinkers, strategists, coders, surveillance experts, tech geeks and disruptors to utilise all of the tools we have available to us to build the world that we want to see. A world where black lives matter. A world where all lives matter.'

Identify three things which would help achieve your objective, for example, 'I need my local MP to...'

_____

_____

_____

106

Tip

Think about writing an opinion piece to raise a topic that a mainstream outlet may not have paid enough attention to, then pitch it to print and online newspapers – or post it on your own social media accounts.

'When we speak we are afraid our words will not
be heard or welcomed. But when we are silent, we
are still afraid. So it is better to speak.'
Audre Lorde

Once you've created your key message, it's time to campaign
to raise awareness and educate people about the issue. This
can also increase public pressure on decision-makers and,
hopefully, start a public debate about your cause.

Some possible methods include: marches, public exhibitions, high-profile stunts, performances, music concerts, petitions, public meetings and strikes. Making the world a better place won't happen overnight, and it might take some time to see any progress. It isn't easy, but fear not, it will be worth it.

Finally, if you need any more inspiration, then another campaigning role model you should be aware of is Olive Morris, a black rights community activist and campaigner in South London in the 1970s. She co-founded the Brixton Black Women's Group, the first black women's group in the UK, in 1973. Olive was a radical black feminist who bravely organised anti-racist marches and used her voice to speak up against racial, sexual and class oppression. She played a key role in the Black Panther movement in the UK and in the squatter movement, and has left an amazing legacy of activism for us all to build on.

'Luck has nothing to do with it, because I have spent many, many hours, countless hours, on the court working for my one moment in time, not knowing when it would come.'

Serena Williams

Black women are at an immediate disadvantage in the workplace, because we do not look or sound like the people who overwhelmingly make up the majority of today's business leaders – white men.

Vanessa Kingori explains in *Slay In Your Lane* why we should embrace visibility rather than fight it:

'If I'm in a situation where I'm sitting in a room, there's no point pretending that I'm less visible; I have to be aware of that and then I have to make good of it. But I think it's such an advantage, because if you think about it, there are many business books written about trying to be noticed, trying to get cut through, trying to get your bosses' attention, trying to whatever. We celebrate that in our work and our output, right? So it's like, "I want to be noticed." We have that in our physicality, rightly or wrongly, there's no point fighting it. It just is what it is, but use it as an advantage.'

We've all heard the saying, 'Your network is your net worth.' This is not limited to money, but includes skills, knowledge and access to opportunities. In this section we will help you celebrate your career highs to date, level up your skills and help you identify some new career goals.

Studies have shown that ethnic minorities who advance the furthest in their careers all share one asset: a strong network of mentors and sponsors who nurture their professional development. Knowing the difference and taking advantage of it could really make an impact on your career progression.

'I am not lucky. You know what I am? I am smart, I am talented, I take advantage of the opportunities that come my way and I work really, really hard. Don't call me lucky. Call me a badass.'
Shonda Rhimes, Year of Yes: How to Dance It Out, Stand In the Sun and Be Your Own Person

Multi-award-winning senior lawyer and diversity leader in the UK, Funke Abimbola, calls this the triumvirate in *Slay In Your Lane*:

'Sponsorship, mentoring and coaching are the three things that are essential to career progression, and they're all very different. Mentoring is guidance and advice. Sponsoring is someone actively looking for opportunities for you and putting you forward for them. Coaching is actually teaching you the skills: how to influence; how to communicate; how to get by; this is how you should run the meeting and so on. All three have been absolutely essential for my career progression.'

Now, take a few moments to go online to find a job description of the role you think you would like to have next in your career. What is it about this role that appeals to you the most?

_____

_____

_____

Tip

Before you complete this section, it might be helpful to complete the personal brand exercise on page 86.

Now, thinking about your own personal brand (see pages 88), what value and unique perspective can you bring to the role?

_____

_____

_____

What skills included in the job description are you currently missing?

_____

_____

_____

Top three skills I am known for today:

_____

_____

_____

Top three skills I want to be known for in the future:

_____

_____

_____

*'The only thing that separates women of colour
from anyone else, is opportunity.'*
Viola Davis

**What are the three biggest career goals you've achieved so
far in your life?**

_____

_____

_____

113

What makes these special to you?

_____

_____

_____

My short-term career goal is:

_____

_____

_____

Why is it important to you?

_____

_____

_____

'We should each be CEO of our own board of directors.'
Vanessa Kingori

As you move towards your career goals you will need to draw upon your own network of people to help you at different points on your journey. *Slay In Your Lane* would not have been possible without a network of people we were able to reach out to and ask for help in the initial stages. The fact is, you have to network in order to build a successful career, but it's also the case that a great way to get inspired is to get out there and network with like-minded people. It will require you to step out of your comfort zone (again!) and engage in new activities, to attend events and meet new people, but it is a sure-fire way of creating opportunities for you, as well as many potential rewards.

We all have people we trust and can confide in. Who makes up your own personal board of directors at the moment?

_____

_____

_____

_____

Is there anyone else you'd like to be on it?

_____

_____

_____

_____

How will you go about approaching them?

_____

_____

_____

Irene Agbontaen, founder of clothing brand TTYA (Taller Than Your Average), explains: 'Social media's a nice entry-level platform, but then you need to actually go and meet people, and say, "Can we have a coffee? We have similar ideas, let's connect."' But authenticity here is key. Irene says: 'When you have ulterior motives of, "Oh, I'm only going to be friends with this person because they're going to get me into here," or, "They're seen as this," it's not authentic, it doesn't work out. So work on building authentic relationships.'

Now make a list of five other people you'd like to engage or simply connect with:

_____

_____

_____

_____

_____

Tip

Follow them on social media, get to know their interests through their work. Go to events they're going to be at, introduce yourself and your work and go from there!

Tip

Building a powerful network doesn't require you to be an expert at networking. It just requires you to be an expert at something. It is this expertise that forms the basis of trust in your networking relationships.

'If you want the performance I can bring, you're going to pay me what I deserve.'
Taraji P. Henson

One of the most important things to be aware of as you progress in your career is your earning potential. How do you make sure you are maximising your qualifications and work experience so you can work towards a career that's going to pay you enough to live the life you want to live?

Talking about money on a good day is hard enough, but negotiating your salary can be a whole other beast in itself. However, it is essential that we negotiate our salaries at every opportunity to make sure we are asking for what we deserve. Performance ratings are a key part of this process: they are an opportunity to illustrate to your manager what you've achieved that year.

Ratings affect promotions and pay rises, so it is important that your manager takes note of you and is exposed to the work you have done throughout the year.

As the saying goes, *'You don't get what you deserve, you get what you negotiate.'*

'Be an expert. Be brilliant, bold and brave and know your industry inside out; know how it works and know the history and the culture, and just know it and breathe it and live it.'

Sharmaine Lovegrove

Tip

Get in touch with recruiters; they can help assess your CV and where you are situated within the market rate. Go to LinkedIn and GlassDoor to check the salary range that a person with similar experience to you could expect to earn. Arming yourself with this information will give you a perspective on and the confidence about what it is realistic to ask for.

Use this space to write a short introductory email to them

117

Tip

Keep it short but sweet. Introduce yourself (including your personal brand), explain why you are writing to them, acknowledge that they are very busy but if they had time in the future to meet somewhere that is convenient for them, to talk about XYZ, you'd be immensely grateful.

So how do you go about this?

1. Firstly, do your research and update your CV.

2. Next, book a meeting with your manager and let them know in advance what the meeting is about: no one likes being caught off guard.

3. When you have the meeting, don't get personal, discuss the facts. Rather than saying, 'I'm worth X,' be as objective as possible and instead approach it by saying, 'After researching it, I can see that someone of my experience is paid in the range of X amount.'

4. Highlight specific examples of how you have demonstrated your experience and expertise in the work you have done. This is no time to be modest. Black women have to provide more evidence of competence than their white counterparts in the workplace.

What part of your job have you done amazingly well?

_____

_____

_____

_____

What challenges have you dealt well with since your last review?

_____

_____

_____

5. You should outline your accomplishments in a factual manner. You might find it easier to do this by using numbers and data. Come prepared with specific examples of how you have contributed to the business's objectives.

6. Practise, practise, practise. In *Slay In Your Lane*, Dr Anne-Marie Imafidon advises: 'Always practise your negotiation – with a friend, with a mentor, with your mum, with your dad. If you've said it out loud, and you've practised that thing, then it's a lot easier for you to go into negotiation, because you kind of already know what could happen or not, so it's not a new thing for you.'

And finally...sometimes even the best laid plans go awry.

There may be some instances when you're not being compensated fairly: when, even though you are working twice as hard and trying to take advantage of your visibility, it isn't reflected in your progressing to the next level in your career. This can be really frustrating, and it may then be that it is time to look elsewhere.

Dr Anne-Marie agrees: 'If those people don't recognise it, it's one of those things. That door may be closed; another will be open elsewhere, and you have to knock on those doors, and you might think it's because you're black, you might think it's because you're young, you might think it's because you're a woman, but none of that matters; there's a door that'll be open for you somewhere else because you are those things, but you have to go and find that door; don't be knocking on a door that's not going to value you.'

Tip

Go into it knowing how much you want and what is the lowest amount you will accept. The worst thing you can do is settle for an amount you're really not comfortable with, because it will only store up resentment down the line.

Tip

It's a good idea to make a habit of recording your achievements in a document (or a journal like this one!) that will help you measure your impact throughout the year: try not wait until the last minute.

"So I feel at this time the platforms are open, every-thing in terms of society, social media, culture, music, arts, fashion, everything's kind of just aligned now. So this is the time for us to really just grasp it and move forward."

Irene Agbontaen

Your particular story and your individual perspective on life is an invaluable asset: one that many of us often fail to recognise. The opportunities for black women to make money from what we know have never been more abundant, and more and more of us are taking advantage of technology to create podcasts, online platforms and e-commerce sites.

120

But while you may have an idea for a potential side hustle or business, taking that leap of faith and transforming it into a product or service is where the real challenge lies. Because life gets in the way, right? However, if you have a good idea, there are more opportunities than ever to create your own lane and build something great from the ground up. Now could be the perfect time for you to start a side hustle or passion project.

1. Name an entrepreneur you admire: _____

2. What about them inspires you? _____

1.

2.

STEP 1: NOW LET'S DETERMINE YOUR WHY

The motivation to create a side hustle can spring from the most surprising places, and for a variety of reasons. In *Slay In Your Lane*, entrepreneur Florence Adepoju told us she was inspired to start her hip-hop-inspired cosmetic line because she wanted to create a beauty brand that was inclusive for all women and to address the lack of representation in mainstream brands.

This lack of representation presents an opportunity for black entrepreneurs to take matters into their own hands and create products and services that actively solve the problems they, and two million others in the UK alone, face.

Whatever your own personal reason for why you want to start a side hustle – maybe it's for the extra spending money or because you want to be your own boss – it can offer you flexibility, greater job satisfaction and the opportunity to make a difference to other people's lives.

Your **why** is what will keep you going when things don't necessarily go to plan and you want to give up. So it's the most important place to start. What do you want to accomplish by starting a side hustle? Think about your WHY and finish these sentences:

1. I'm starting a side hustle because... _____

2. So that I can... _____

Tip

Your side hustle should inspire you, motivate you and most importantly excite you!

1. _____

_____

_____

_____

2. _____

_____

_____

_____

Tip

Will this side hustle make the best use of my skills?

STEP 2: FIND YOUR IDEA

So, you have the drive and want to start a business, but you haven't had that light-bulb moment yet? You're not alone, and if this is you, and you are just missing a killer idea, you should begin by exploring your passions and interests – spend time discovering what it is that you truly care about.

Starting a business is challenging, and inevitably your commitment will be tested, so you're more likely to commit and be motivated to stick it out if it has its roots in something you're passionate about.

124

1. Think about your hobbies, what do you like doing? List them on the opposite page:

2. What are you passionate about?

Now that we've established what you're passionate about and what you like doing, let's think about your skill set because the right side hustle will need to complement your skills and abilities. Think about your strengths and what you do well. Be honest with yourself. This is an opportunity to see what experience you already have and how it can help you.

3. List your top three strengths:

Now it's time to use your passion and skill set to see how you can mould this into a side hustle idea and solve a real problem people might be currently experiencing.

4. Note down three everyday problems in your life that you would like to solve:

Tip

This will also later help you spot what you're missing when you decide on your idea. There might be areas that you are not skilled in and this will help you identify the gaps prior to an issue arising.

1.

2.

3.

4.

Now think about the industries associated with these problems (for example, fashion, health, technology). Do some research into them. Has anyone else spotted the problems you've identified? Have they tried to solve them? If not, or if they haven't managed to solve them, then you might have found your niche.

For example, in 2013, entrepreneur Tristan Walker launched Bevel, a technologically advanced shaving system for black men. He saw an opportunity in the billion-dollar personal-care market and decided to start a business he was already an expert in. Armed with the knowledge that people of colour tend to have curly hair, and when they shave with multi-blade razors they're more likely to get razor bumps, skin irritation and ingrown hairs, Tristan created the single-blade shaving system, Bevel. His entrepreneurial mission was to 'make health and beauty simple for people of colour'.

Think about your target audience and customer and why they would want your idea. Do you think the problem you've identified is one they would want solved too?
Think big! If you could create anything to solve this, what would it be?

1. My side hustle will be:

2. My side hustle will solve:

> Tip
>
> Can this capture the zeitgeist?

Have a think about the commitments you have each week and your usual schedule. How much time do you have available outside of your day job and other commitments to commit to your idea? Be realistic!

I have _____ hours free every week. This could be your new side hustle time! Are you ready to make the commitment into getting this idea off the ground? If so, read on!

1. _____

   _____

   _____

   _____

   _____

2. _____

   _____

   _____

   _____

   _____

Tip

If you're stuck and can't answer this just yet, go back to the start of the exercise. Your idea will need to solve some sort of need because that's how people will determine its value.

STEP 3: RESEARCH

So, you have what you believe to be a great idea to fill a gap in the market, the next big thing. After your initial excitement, the next stage should be the idea-validation process – testing and validating your side hustle before you move any further down the road. You need to find out whether your idea has any legs and whether it offers any real value. It's harsh but true; you don't want to waste time on an idea that nobody wants.

This process will also help you create the best product or service for your potential customers, finding out what they want and whether your business idea meets this demand. It will answer the central question: should I even be starting this side hustle? Validating your idea involves doing market research to identify what problem, want or need your business solves, and exactly how it solves it. It exposes your idea to your target audience before you create and release the final thing.

There are a variety of research methods available for you to use, but to begin with, the internet is probably the cheapest and simplest way of doing market research.

1. What are some of the leading blogs/magazines/publications?

2. Who are the leaders and influencers in the industry?

3. How are people making money in the industry (for example, are they making money through partnerships, sponsored links, ticket sales, etc.)?

4. What are the leading organisations and businesses in the space?

1.

2.

3.

4.

'You can compete or you can collaborate', who can help you bring your idea to life?

Although with *Slay In Your Lane* we really believed in the idea from the jump and knew that there was an obvious need and market for it, we still made sure we did our market research. We wanted feedback, so we set up a focus group to better understand our demographic and what their interests were.

We took a field-based approach with our market research, but others, like Irene, used social media. Through asking questions on Facebook and online survey tools, she was able to find out in a pretty short space of time whether her business idea met a need, and whether there was a clear demand for her potential product.

Irene explains: 'I put out a post on Facebook, just using SurveyMonkey®, asking, "Can people fill out this survey for me and let me know what your feeling is on fashion for tall women?" I got over a thousand responses just from Facebook, and then I thought, "Do you know what? This could actually be a good idea." Then I started doing all my market research; I looked at my competitors and saw that there wasn't actually a cool, jersey, staple apparel for tall girls – everything associated with tall fashion was kind of always frumpy, not really on trend, you know? So it was really important to me to make the girl who's always felt excluded, included.'

As well as market research, it is vital that you also do competitor research. This will be key to understanding your unique selling point. You need to ask yourself, what else is out there? What is going to be unique, compelling or different about my idea? Does it meet the needs of an underserved group? Or fill a real gap in the market? Can I make something a little better, cheaper and faster? Don't worry if someone is out there doing something similar; look at what they're doing and decide whether you can offer something better.

Your unique selling point is the heart of your business idea: the point of differentiation is that it will help you to stand out from the crowd. It is the reason why your potential customer will choose you over anyone else. You should spend time working on this and really understanding the strengths of your idea. It's what will give you a competitive advantage in a crowded market place. As Steve Jobs famously said, 'You don't have to be the first, but you've got to be the best.'

Now you have a better sense of the market and your competition, you can focus on really looking at what niches aren't being served in the market. And you can think about ways you can improve, disrupt or turn this industry upside down.

Tip

Using survey tools such as Typeform and SurveyMonkey, you can create and send out surveys to your contacts, allowing you to gauge if people are attracted to your idea

You've done your research and identified your USP. Now you need to make it part of your brand vision. This vision should encapsulate your end goal: an aspirational statement that paints a picture of what you want to achieve with your brand in the future. If you've done the personal branding exercises on pages 86-95 you will see how the same techniques can be applied to your side hustle idea. When she first started WAH, standing out from the crowd by being at the forefront of technology was key for Sharmadean Reid:

'The internet's completely responsible for why we dominated in nail art. I constantly blogged and posted on Facebook – because there was no Instagram then so we had a WAH blog, we had a WAH page on Facebook, and I would just always be posting all the work we did, but also all the activities around the salon.

'A brand isn't literally about their output, it's about all the things that happen pre, during and post the output – so it's about the girls who come into the salon, it's about the nails being done, it's about the end result of the nails happening, and I think I just shared every bit of the journey online, whereas other people were maybe just showing the nails. Instead, I built a story around it.'

One of your greatest challenges as an entrepreneur will be to create a unique vision that sets your business apart from the rest. For example, Bill Gates wanted to put 'a computer on every desk and in every home'. Sharmadean Reid wanted to have the 'coolest salon ever', and with *Slay In Your Lane* our vision was to create 'a guide to life for a generation of black

British women: The Black Girl Bible'.

The best ideas are simple and clear to communicate, which is why you need to perfect your elevator pitch – a short, pre-prepared statement that includes why your brand is here, what it stands for and what it aims to achieve.

1. What is your brand vision?

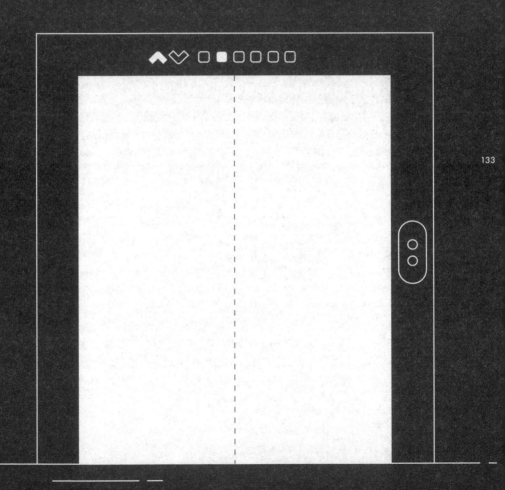

BUSINESS PLAN

'I felt there was a girl like me, who was always excluded, and I wanted to make that excluded girl feel included.'
Irene Agbontaen

Once you have established your USP and your brand vision, you need to complete a business plan: a written document that describes your objectives and strategies, helps you understand the type of business you want to build, the action plan you will need to follow, and which includes sales, marketing and financial forecasts.

134

This plan is essential if you want to be successful; it's a valuable roadmap for launching and growing your business – after all, failing to plan is planning to fail. Your business plan should be strategic.

Ideas are plentiful but a business plan will help you identify potential weaknesses and opportunities that will help you make informed decisions before you and your investors commit financially and legally. There are several free business plan templates available online. We like this one, by the Prince's Trust: *https://www.princes-trust.org.uk/help-for-young-people/tools-resources/business-tools/business-plans*

Procrastination is a bitch. It is all too easy to theorise an idea and refine it in your head a million times instead of actually taking that initial step. Starting is always the hardest part: it can be daunting and, as we saw in Chapter Two, analysis paralysis can all too often leave us frozen by overthinking.

But don't let the fear of failure hold you back. You have to ask yourself whether your desire to do something is greater than your fear of attempting to do it. You will need to draw on all your reserves of self-confidence to take the huge step of starting a side hustle.

When Beyoncé was nine, she competed in Star Search, an American talent show. The prize on offer was a recording contract. Great, right? She noted: 'In my mind we would perform on Star Search, we would win, we would get a record deal...there was no way in the world that I would have ever imagined losing as a possibility,' (from mini-documentary *Self-Titled: Part 2. Imperfection* posted to YouTube in 2013).

Her group, Girl's Tyme, didn't win the competition but it taught Beyoncé a valuable lesson.

'The reality is, sometimes you lose. And you're never too good to lose, you're never too big to lose, you're never too smart to lose, it happens. And it happens when it needs to happen. And you have to embrace those things.'

It's all about embracing challenges, having the courage to commit and persevere, and always being aware of the bigger picture and the difference that your product or service can make, big or small. It requires creative thinking, determination, the capacity to take risks, leadership, and, of course, passion. The stakes tend to be high, the bumps in the road frequent. Remaining focused, regardless of the obstacles, is paramount. But the reward could be the chance to create something really special!

List of resources to help you get started:

www.virginstartup.org
www.startups.co.uk
www.princes-trust.org.uk
www.fastcompany.com
www.bteg.co.uk
www.squarespace.com
www.wordpress.com
www.typeform.com
www.surveymonkey.co.uk
www.startupbritain.org
www.generalassemb.ly
www.campus.co/london/en
www.startuploans.co.uk
www.enterprisenation.com
www.greatbusiness.gov.uk/women-in-enterprise
www.bl.uk/business-and-ip-centre
www.futuregirlscorp.com

'In the black community, [depression is] something that happens, but we don't speak about it. We have to continue to talk about it and bring it straight to the forefront.'

Letitia Wright

Black women's 'strength' is a double-edged sword. Our resilience help us to thrive when the odds are stacked against us, and to make our way over hurdles with perceived ease. But 'perceived' is the operative word.

This same strength can lead people to believe that we are immune to any slight or obstacle that comes our way, and as a consequence, any acknowledgement of emotional trauma is read as 'weakness'. Because of this, it's important every now and again to check in with yourself. How do you feel at the beginning and end of each day? Chart your week on a scale of 1–5 in terms of your mood in the morning and evening for a clearer picture of how you feel.

1 = Happy; 2 = Content; 3 = Okay; 4 = Indifferent; 5 = Unhappy

	Morning	Evening
Monday		
Tuesday		
Wednesday		
Thursday		
Friday		
Saturday		
Sunday		

What have you learnt about how you're really doing? When do you feel your best and why? When were you at your lowest and do you have a sense of why? Jot down some possible reasons below:

_____

_____

_____

Can you spot a pattern? Is it a pattern you feel you might be able to change, or that you might need to seek help to change?

A therapist Yomi once had offered her a simple but useful analogy: that several straws were going into her from different avenues – work, relationships, money, family – sapping away her mental and physical energy, and because she never sought support, she was never replenished. She simply continued until she completely dried out, and was unable to be of use to anyone around her or to herself.

As 'strong black women', we often fall into the trap of believing we can bring ourselves out of every and any thing, but we also need the care, support and strength that we readily give to others. In order to be helpful to our loved ones, we have to love ourselves and ensure we are okay, too.

What are the things that are taking it out of you? Label them here.

Now, what are the things that replenish you? Label them here.

It can be tough remaining positive, with so much going on, and pretending things are perfect definitely doesn't make them so. So it's important to have a form of release. All the negative thoughts, feelings and things in or around you, let them out in the thought bubbles below. Don't hold back and be honest with yourself.

142

Good. Now, let's see how we can turn these negative thoughts and feelings into something more positive. What can you do to change these things, if anything? What can you do to change your attitude towards these things?

I feel like everyone around me is succeeding and I'm not I should be inspired by their success and see it as proof dreams can come true

When you're in a bad space, feeling better is often about taking each day as it comes and as best as you can. We should do what we can, when we can, especially when it comes to pressing tasks, where we start with smaller, more manageable things until we're capable of properly doing the slightly bigger things. Looking after your mental health often also involves simply slowing down or sometimes stopping altogether, if you're able to. Yomi had to take time out of university in order to get herself back on track, but that wouldn't be necessary for everyone; sometimes a few days off spent taking care of yourself, recharging and resting, can do a great deal, or at least help clarify in your mind about what steps you should take next.

Here are 31 tips for each day in the month to help you get in the habit of slowing down at least once a day:

1. Read for an hour, uninterrupted.

2. Unplug for two hours. Switch everything to airplane mode and free yourself from the constant noise of social media and email.

3. Take another, more scenic route to work.

4. Take a bubble bath – complete with candles and calming music.

5. Take a leisurely walk without a specific destination in mind.

6. Meditate for 20 minutes.

7. Play a board game with loved ones.

8. Make and put on a homemade face mask.

9. Try a pillow spray – you don't have to buy a specific sleep spray, the main thing is that you enjoy the scent.

10. Do something crafty: colouring, knitting, sewing, etc.

11. Revisit a favourite thing from your childhood.

12. Sit in the grass and watch the clouds float by.

13. Look at the stars.

14. Take a mental health day off work or uni or college – and feel not an ounce of guilt about it.

15. Give yourself a pedicure or a manicure.

16. Sit in a coffee shop and sip on a luxurious drink.

17. Do yoga.

18. Close yourself in a room and listen to the latest episode of your favourite podcast.

19. Have a 20-minute stretching session.

20. Go swimming (for fun, not exercise).

21. Go to bed early.

22. Declutter a spot in your house that's been annoying you.

23. Write a list of 'annoying tasks' that have been weighing on you and complete them in an hour.

24. Watch the sun rise or set. Don't take any pictures or post about it on social media. Just watch.

25. Research something that you've been interested in but haven't had the time to dive into.

26. Edit who you follow on social media (if they make you feel bad about life or yourself, get rid).

27. Go to a museum: art, children's, history, science – whatever!

28. Write a letter (or an email) to an old friend.

29. Take yourself on a self-date. Spend an hour alone doing something that makes you happy.

30. Say 'no' to someone.

31. Start a bucket list.

'I have a very good personal life. I understand that it's the internet but I'm married with a baby. I'm very happy, so I try and keep my focus on those things that are important to me, which is my family, my baby. That's what's important to me. I mean, it can sting for a moment and then I bring everything back into perspective to what's important to me.'

Patricia Bright

Social media can take its toll in many ways: the constant negative news cycle, trolling and the never-ending comparison to those who seem to be happier, more successful and better looking. Patricia Bright, a lifestyle YouTuber and entrepreneur, uses her platform for work, too, and her role as an influencer requires her to be online far more than average. Yet even she is sure to focus on what matters offline, in order to put things into perspective.

The internet is truly a tale of two cities. Trolls want black women with opinions – hell, just black women being black women – to be driven off the internet for good, and very little is being done to give us an incentive to stay. Here's hoping that the internet we love so much finally does something for us in return and makes itself, and ultimately us, safer. Until then though, it's important to practise self-care and ensure you prioritise your well-being when online.

Here are some tips to help with staying sane on the internet:

1. Have a friend change your password (works wonders if you're on deadline and need to focus).

2. Delete the worst offending apps from your phone. If you really do need to log into Twitter or Facebook, simply do so on your desktop.

3. Curate your feed so that you're only following a few people you actually care about and don't make you feel bad.

4. Turn off notifications on your phone.

5.   Download apps which track how much time you spend online each day. This will hopefully encourage you to change how you spend your day offline as well as online.

6.   Ban phones at bedtime. (You can get an old-fashioned alarm clock – no excuses!)

7.   Prioritise one platform rather than being everywhere. Think critically about what works for you and why, not what you're most addicted to.

8.   If you've tried taking breaks from social media and actually liked it, consider getting rid of your account completely and deactivate. You've lived without it before...

9.   Go cold turkey: the most difficult option, but can also work wonders for your mental health.

The stigma around mental illness paralyses people in the black community from opening up about mental health, but when we do, often the only remedy prescribed to us is scripture. But if we can acknowledge that most medical treatments were created to help God's people, why not therapy.

Use this space to write down five 'prayers'.

If you're not religious, then write down five of your hopes, or fears, or anxieties.

_____

_____

_____

_____

_____

If you think about it, prayer is often a form of therapy and when you think about it further, these are things that you can discuss both with God and a therapist. VV Brown is from a Christian family, and whilst prayer gave her strength, the fact it was touted as the only solution to her mental health problems also left her depression sidelined for some time:

'I was raised in the church where every single cure was "Pray about it", right? Now I'm not saying that prayer doesn't work, because I was raised in church and I do believe in the power of prayer,

that's my belief. But I also believe that it's more than prayer and some things are psychological. And I think because a lot of black families are rooted in church, we ignore the psychological aspect and we don't talk about it. There's almost a stigma of shame when you talk about mental illness, and not a real understanding of it.'
VV Brown

'Fitness is definitely changing my life, I'll admit a lot of my motivation has been in the past – and there's still the dregs of it there – about getting down to some ridiculous size and feeling like Naomi Campbell or something. More now it's about [how] I can feel, how my body is stronger, and so mentally I feel better and better equipped to deal with the days and events.'
Laura Mvula

And finally...Don't forget that your mental health is linked to your physical health. Both are paramount to feeling like the best version of you. There are several ways you can keep fit and active: a local class, taking up boxing (on YouTube if you can't face a class), swimming or even just a brisk walk.

According to the NHS, to stay healthy or improve health, adults need to do two types of physical activity each week: aerobic and strength exercises. It is recommended adults between the ages of 19 and 64 do 150 minutes of moderate aerobic activity such as cycling or brisk walking every week and strength exercises on two or more days a week that work all the major muscles (so, your legs, hips, back, abdomen, chest, shoulders and arms).

Sponsor yourself to do something sporty! In the table below, fill out a sporting goal in one column. And then a reward for yourself for completing it:

SPORTING GOAL	REWARD
Swim ten lengths	
Run one mile...	
Ride your bike to the corner shop	

When it comes to our emotional and mental well-being we can share the load through faith, therapy and friends. The latter can be the hardest but as musician Laura Mvula, who was formally diagnosed with clinical depression and sought treatment last year, says in *Slay In Your Lane*, she believes the first step to breaking the stigma around mental health in the black community is conversation:

'I've been so overwhelmed with the feeling of being charged with a new responsibility to just expose that stigma. It's so old-fashioned, that's the other thing. It's outdated. We are mind, body and soul, it's so basic. Maybe there needs a balance to be struck, but I think for the most part I don't think you can be too vulnerable with trustworthy people.'
Laura Mvula

'Being a healthy woman isn't about getting on a scale or measuring your waistline. We need to start focusing on what matters – on how we feel, and how we feel about ourselves.'

Michelle Obama

Being busy and building an empire is often seen as winning at life. But too often our pursuit of success can compromise our health.

It's important to go to the doctor when you notice changes in your body. In 2006, Vannessa Amadi was working on various different projects in her PR career and started to feel very stressed:

'It's hard to put your health first. I had found a lump in my neck when I was about 24 and I just felt it was nothing at first, and it was actually vanity that made me go and check it out properly because it was growing and I thought, I don't want a big old lump hanging out my neck. That's the only reason I went to the doctor, and thank God I did, it turned out to be cancerous and I had to have treatment.'

The lump turned out to be Hodgkin's lymphoma and her doctor told her it was related to the excessive stress she had been under. She was very lucky to catch it when she did.

According to Cancer Research UK, black women in England are almost twice as likely to be diagnosed with advanced breast cancer compared to white women.

Low awareness of symptoms and screening (meaning abnormal cells or tumours are found at a later, more advanced stage) is one of the key issues.

Black women are also less likely than white women to go for a mammogram when invited by the NHS. Spotting the early signs of cancer is very important, as the sooner it's detected and treated, the better the outcome.

Try to get into the habit of checking your breasts once a month to familiarise yourself with how your breasts normally look and feel. Examine yourself several days after your period ends, when your breasts are least likely to be swollen and tender. Look out for these signs.

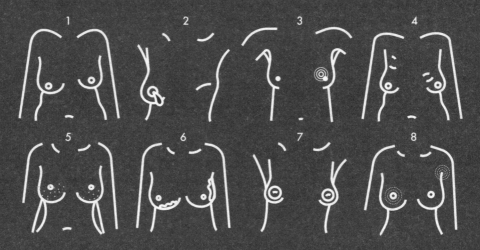

1. Change in size or shape.
2. Discharge from nipple, without squeezing.
3. Redness or rash around skin/nipple.
4. Lump or thickening that feels different from rest of breast tissue.
5. Change in skin texture such as puckering, dimpling (like the skin of an orange).
6. Swelling in armpit/around collarbone.
7. Nipple becoming inverted or changing shape/position.
8. Pain in breast or armpit that's always there.

ask yourself: when you received your cervical screening invitation, did you go? Did your first cervical cancer screening happen at the age of 25? If not, book your cervical screening with your GP now.

Here is a quick list of what you should be checking:

- [ ] Cervical smear (every three years)

- [ ] Check breasts (once a month)

- [ ] STI check (once every three to six months, dependent on relationship status)
- [ ] General physical (every two to three years)

HEALTH IS WEALTH!

A study published by the University of Georgia, in the US, found that 'white blood cells among the strivers were prematurely aged relative to those of their peers' and suggested that black youths with an 'unrelenting determination to succeed' were more likely than their white peers to get sick or contract illnesses in the process of working towards their goal.

White Americans, in the study, seemed relatively immune to the negative effects of the pursuit for success. This is not because they are naturally more resilient, but because due to white privilege, they don't have to be as resilient.

So, for starters, you should make sure you are able to get that minimum of six hours or more of sleep a night, rather than relying upon coffee and caffeine-laden energy drinks. Track your sleep and water consumption for the month. Use the trackers on page 40.

Pretty Hurts

Black women's hair products are more likely to contain hazardous chemicals. To say 'Pretty hurts' would be putting it mildly, how about 'Pretty kills?' The cocktail of chemicals used in relaxers and hair dyes reads like an ingredients list for a DIY chemical bomb. Relaxers are laced with corrosive chemicals like sodium hydroxide – used in drain cleaners – and women who have been exposed to them for prolonged periods have been known to develop ailments such as cancer, asthma and fibroids.

The dangers to our health, masked by our cosmetics culture, are insidious, and products that have been a staple in the black girl haircare regime contain higher levels of toxins, steroids and hormone-disrupting chemicals than cosmetics made for non-black women.

Write down what's listed on the back of your top five favourite hair and skin products. Now, search the web and swap it out for a handmade or store-bought organic alternative, then document how your hair/skin fares after a fortnight.

OUT WITH THE OLD	IN WITH THE NEW	RESULT
Ex: Brand deep conditioner – ingredients include	Vinegar and egg conditioner (ingredients: eggs, olive oil, honey, vinegar and lemon juice)	

The more you know about your hair, the better you can learn what works for it. It's very useful to know your hair type and porosity. Porosity refers to how well your hair is able to absorb and hold moisture. Knowing your hair's porosity can help you choose the right products to keep your hair well-moisturised, supple, strong and shiny.

Use the 'float test' method to find out how porous your hair is.
Take a few strands of hair from your comb and drop them into
a bowl of water. Let them sit for two to four minutes. If your
hair floats, you have low porosity. If it sinks, you have high
porosity. Determining your hair type is also a starting point to
finding the right products and styles. Hair stylist Andre Walker
designed a method to help better identify your curls through
the classification method below. Tick which one you are:

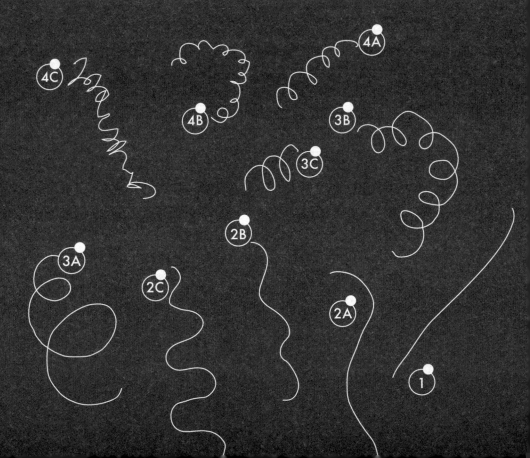

AND DON'T FORGET...

Black people are the most likely to suffer from blood-related diseases such as sickle cell, diabetes and hypertension – conditions that often require blood transfusions and in the case of diabetes can also lead to organ transplants.

But we as a community are not donating enough blood. This is critical because people with sickle cell, as well as other blood-related illnesses, rely upon regular blood transfusions (every three to four weeks for sickle cell sufferers) to be able to live an ordinary life. In addition, stem cell and bone marrow replacement treatments are also used to treat blood-related diseases. At the moment only 1 per cent of black people in the UK are active donors (roughly 10,000 people), which means that fewer people are registered donors than suffer from sickle cell alone. Here's another sobering stat: only 20 out of 1,282 people who passed away in 2015 were registered as black organ donors, even though there are 600 people on the waiting list.

We must solve this amongst ourselves, as similar blood types are more likely to be found within ethnicities, and because certain rare blood types in black people can only be found within those of the same ethnic background. As it stands, the lack of organs and blood available currently means that black people have only a 20 per cent chance of finding a suitable match from an unrelated donor. Sign up at https://my.blood.co.uk/preregister to donate blood today.

'If someone doesn't make you feel like you can take over the world, then they're not the person for you.'

Charlene White

Slaying in your own lane doesn't mean you need to be on your own to do it. In fact, it's having the support of other people, whether friends, partners or family, that gives us the strength to slay in our lanes. Relationships, of all kinds, matter in ensuring we reach our full potential and thrive in our every goal. For any of us, the pressure to find 'the one' is made even worse by the expectations that society has about women and marriage.

'Because I am female, I am expected to aspire to marriage. I am expected to make my life choices always keeping in mind that marriage is the most important.'
Chimamanda Ngozi Adichie

As women, no matter how much we may achieve or contribute to the world, a great many people still believe that the most important thing we can do is get married, settle down and raise beautiful babies. The dreaded 'When will you marry?' question from parents, aunts, uncles and even acquaintances can ruin a birthday party, BBQ or christening, so it's best to be prepared for the inevitable interrogation.

WHEN WILL YOU MARRY?

Here are some creative responses that should hopefully put nosy relatives off asking for some time. Add your own responses at the end:

- 'On the 30th February!'
- 'There is a large decline in divorce rates if I get married between the ages of 25 to 29 and even lower between the ages of 30 to 34.'
- 'Around the same time I can expect another niece/ nephew!'
- 'The day you actually resist the urge to ask this question!'
- 'I'm still holding out for Michael B Jordan.'
- 'You'll know when I know!'
- 'When you write me the blank cheque!'
- _____
- _____
- _____
- _____

'I think a lot of women feel that pressure, but I think it's an individual choice. You know, I'm not one of these people who says, "Don't have kids at 25," or whatever. Do what feels right. If you're a woman who actually just wants to get married and have kids, that's cool. If you're a woman who wants to have a career, that's cool, too. It's up to you, it's what feels authentic, and for me the choices I've made feel authentic.'

June Sarpong

As it's not women who traditionally do the asking and therefore the 'choosing', we often forget that marriage is a choice. Society can make us feel that our worth is only measured by the value placed upon us by someone who chooses to marry us. But in an ideal world we would have our own agency and free will to make what is nothing less than a life-changing decision as part of a two-way process.

Marriage can be a beautiful thing and a source of mutual support. Marriage is a life choice, but it's not the only choice, and it's not necessarily a better one either: just a different one. If we let ourselves be coerced into seeing marriage as the ultimate goal and pin our hopes, dreams and ambitions on this one thing, then there's a danger that if it doesn't happen for us, we will think it's because we're not good enough. We need to remember that it isn't the be-all and end-all of womanhood.

'I have never gotten so much approval and accolades and warmth and congratulations as when I had a guy on my arm that people thought I was going to marry. Nobody congratulated me that hard when I had my three children. Nobody congratulated me that hard when I won a Golden Globe or a Peabody or my 14 NAACP Image Awards. But when I had a guy on my arm that people thought I was going to marry, people lost their minds like Oprah was giving away cars. I was fascinated by it because I thought, like, I am not Dr Frankenstein, I didn't make this guy – he just is there. Everything else I actually had something to do with.'
Shonda Rhimes

- *Beyoncé – married at 27, first child at 30*
- *Serena Williams – married at 36, first child at 36*
- *Rihanna – unmarried, having the time of her life*
- *Janet Jackson – married 3 times, first child at 50*
- *Oprah – never married partner of over 30 years, doesn't have children*

Everyone's relationship journey is different!

LOVING YOURSELF

Patriarchy has tied a woman's worth almost entirely to her outward appearance, so our relationship prospects are immediately contingent on perceived desirability. This is something that sucks for all women. It sucks even more, however, when the concept of what is beautiful and desirable has been created in total juxtaposition to what you are.

As Patricia Hill Collins put it in *Black Feminist Thought*, 'Blue-eyed, blond, thin white women could not be considered classically beautiful without the Other – Black women with classical African features of dark skin, broad noses, full lips, and kinky hair'. As black women, it's important we love the skin we're in in a world that so often tells us we shouldn't. Remind yourself what makes you great, both inside and out, by listing 'a few of my favourite things':

On my face: I really like my

_____

_____

On my body: I love my

_____

_____

About me: I'm very good at

_____

_____

Black women are not beautiful in spite of their blackness but rather because of it. Even more important than this, though, is the fact that beauty is not something that we as black women, or indeed as women, owe the world, and it is not something that makes us more or less deserving of love. Whether you're 4C or 3B, black hair is beautiful. Write your favourite things about your hair in the afro and note what styles you want to try next.

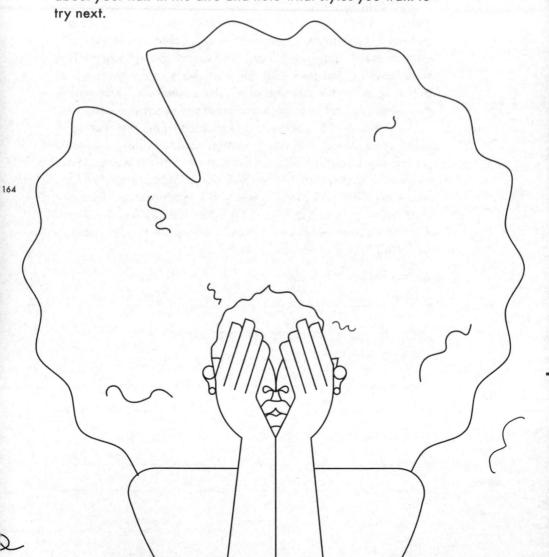

The Obamas, the Carters, the Pinkett-Smiths, the Wilsons and various other couples are often wheeled out on social media as the walking embodiments of when black excellence merges with black love. However, they are also too often used to taunt black women about what we're apparently not – 'If you were a bit more like Michelle maybe you'd catch yourself an Obama!' is a popular quip.

But many forget that after her first year as an associate at Sidley Austin, a 25-year-old Michelle Obama was assigned to mentor summer associate, 27-year-old Barack Obama, by their corporate law firm. She did not dilute herself – she was his boss. Potential partners cannot continue to shout about #BlackExcellence and cower when they meet it.

Fill in the table with all the wonderful traits and qualities you bring to a relationship, of any kind.

Write a shopping list of the five things you thought were non-negotiable when you started dating:

_____

_____

_____

_____

_____

Now, five things you've realised actually matter:

_____

_____

_____

_____

_____

We might make lists of the most desirable attributes for our potential future partner but do we prioritise that they should understand black women's position societally? That they should be 'woke'? Love you for exactly who you are? Be caring? Prioritise the same things as you?

Everyone just wants to be understood by their other half. It cannot be assumed that this is something anyone can do right off the bat. If you had the chance to build your ideal partner, inside and out, what qualities would they have?

Fill in the heart below:

No one is perfect and we all have to start somewhere. But slaying in your relationship is about finding someone who is willing to listen, learn and unlearn – and preferably within their own time and using their own resources. Point those you care enough about towards the things that taught you and hopefully you will grow in awareness together.

So, what matters to you?

Write down the top five most important things/causes/people that are important to you:

_____

_____

_____

_____

_____

'I think I maybe only realised that after I got married actually, how important it was to have somebody that will encourage you, that will support you and – I mean, he reads my press releases, and rewrites them sometimes, and those kinds of things, because he's interested in me winning. I will take that over a six-foot-five guy for sure, I would take that over the guy that drives the Bentley or whatever.'

Vannessa Amadi

We talk about the language of love, but do you know what your love language is? The idea was popularised by Gary Chapman's bestselling book *The Five Love Languages: The Secret to Love That Lasts*. There are five in total:

1. Words of Affirmation: for many, it's important that they are built up by what their partner says. Compliments don't have to be complex – the most heartfelt words are usually the best.

2. Acts of Service: this love language is best summed up as 'actions speak louder than words'. For many, what matters most to them is being taken care of and having their partner do things that are thoughtful and useful to them.

3. Receiving Gifts: this love language is about thoughtful presents making you feel appreciated and loved.

4. Quality Time: if you love to scroll your phone or multi-task whilst talking, you'll likely upset someone whose love language is Quality Time. Dedicating time together without the distractions of apps or Netflix helps you feel comforted in the relationship.

5. Physical Touch: if this is your love language, you feel more close in a relationship through things like holding hands, kissing and hugging.

To ensure you are both getting what you need out of the relationship, find out what your partner's love language is too!

'Behaviour is one thing but I think the bigger signifiers exist in language. I want you to appreciate me and see the beauty of a black woman but there are always those words and killer sentences that immediately let you know you're being fetishised. "Exotic" or "I just loooooove how our skin looks against each other" will always make my eyes roll. I think you just know it in your gut in certain language that is used and how they treat you.'
Clara Amfo

Racial fetishes are often difficult to explain and usually have to be defined on a case by case basis. But one thing is for sure: just because black women don't want to be discarded because they are black, it does not mean they want to be dated because they are black either.

A preference is when your partner values you for yourself, rather than for whatever trait initially drew them to you. Your blackness simply increases their attraction to you. It's not a prerequisite for them to keep finding you attractive: they love you for you, and your Black Magic simply elevates it.

So much of fetishisation is hard to explicitly explain – when you know, you know. You can't go wrong with your gut, but as a handy guide, check out this six-part scale, which ranges from good to very bad...

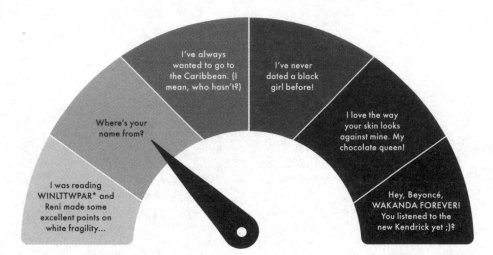

I've always wanted to go to the Caribbean. (I mean, who hasn't?)

I've never dated a black girl before!

Where's your name from?

I love the way your skin looks against mine. My chocolate queen!

I was reading WINLTTWPAR* and Reni made some excellent points on white fragility...

Hey, Beyoncé, WAKANDA FOREVER! You listened to the new Kendrick yet ;)?

Fetishisation strips black women of what actually makes us, us. It relies heavily on assumption and it reduces black women to their skin tone and the several problematic tropes that come along with it.

Be careful out there! But also always remember the most important relationship you have is with yourself. Love of all types is important, but self-love is crucial.

*Why I'm No Longer Talking to White People About Race by Reni Eddo-Lodge

'Is solace anywhere more comforting than that in the arms of a sister?'

Alice Walker

Friendships are hugely important relationships and, frankly, they're underrated. At university, our friendship was a wonderful buffer between us and many things that didn't have nearly the effect on us they might have, had we not had each other. And we could never have foreseen that eight years, several, several hours of phone calls and even more nights out later, we'd be co-writing a book together. Friendships can really be the making of you!

1. Write down a favourite memory of each of your closest friends or family members below. Share it with them afterwards.

    'Having cheerleaders is incredibly important. I think it's really important to have people who are objective, who aren't necessarily in your workplace, who know the real you, the authentic you, who can basically give you a verbal slap when you have those moments, those crises of self-confidence, those moments of lack of self-belief – and we all have them – and you need somebody that's basically going to say, "Why not?" and counsel you through it. And drink lots of wine, if need be, when something's gone wrong.'

    Karen Blackett

1.

THE BLACK GIRL'S GUIDE TO:

FRIENDSHIP

'She is a friend of my mind. She gather me, man. The pieces I am, she gather them and give them back to me in all the right order. It's good, you know, when you got a woman who is a friend of your mind.'

Toni Morrison

1. Name five of your cheerleaders in the pompoms here, and then label each of them with two of their greatest qualities.

2. Now, think about who you're a cheerleader for and list them.

174

3. Are you cheering for everyone who cheers for you? Could you support your cheerleaders more? Think of five things you could do to be a better cheerleader/ supporter for your friends.

1.

2. _____

_____

_____

3. _____

_____

_____

A recent survey of 2,000 people in the UK* looked at people's friendships and the different personality types they fell into. Can spot yourself and your friends in the people described below? Write your/their names next to the corresponding friend type:

1. **The Organiser**

Loves a list and plans everything – organises birthday celebrations, hen parties and holidays, and rallies the troops for a night out.

2. **The Motivator**

Drags you kicking and screaming out of your comfort zone. Whether it's to try a new drink, get a new hobby or try a new hairstyle, you will thank them for it later.

3. **The Oracle**

Knows everything about everything and has been there, and done it too. The person you go to when you need travel tips or advice on the best restaurants.

4. **The Elephant**

Remembers everything: wedding anniversaries, birthdays ...and the time you made fun of their new hair in the groupchat.

5. **The Maverick**

Life and soul of the party. Hands down the best person to rave with, but probably not the most reliable person in your group.

6. **The Scrooge**

Super money-conscious – disappears when it's time to buy drinks but has their phone out to split the bill before you've even finished eating.

7. **Steady Eddie/Edwina**

Your rock. Always there when you need them and the first person you call when things go wrong. No matter what, they've got your back.

*https://www.hfholidays.co.uk/media/assets/
document/asset_files/Which_friend_are_you.pdf

BFFS

'Lots of people want to ride with you in the limo, but what you want is someone who will take the bus with you when the limo breaks down.'

Oprah Winfrey

Many of the most important relationships in our lives are our friendships and it's important not to take them for granted. The best friendships with our best friends are ones where both are valued, respected and understood by each other.

1. Write down your memory of the day you and your best friend first became friends.

2. Write/send each other a question in the morning and give yourselves a day to answer it.

3. Write down something your friend might not know about you.

4. It's your friend's birthday and they're opening their gift from you. Describe their ideal gift.

1.

3.

4.

TOXIC FRIENDS

Not all friendships are created equal. Not all friendships are friendships at all. Some are simply energy and self-esteem drains, masked in mutual interests and shared memories. It's important to check the health of your friendships and, in some cases, work out if they're healthy at all.

So how can you tell if your friend is toxic? Ask yourself these questions and note the answers:

1. How do you feel when your friend's name comes up on the phone when it rings? Negative or positive?

2. Do they respect your boundaries or disregard them?

3. Do they always play the victim?

4. Does your mum like them?

5. Do they celebrate your successes?

6. Do they ever take responsibility when they're wrong?

7. Do they compare you to other, 'better' friends?

8. Do you make all the effort?

9. Do all conversations focus on them?

10. Are you walking on eggshells?

11. Are they jealous of you?

12. Can you trust them?

13. Do they make you feel insecure?

14. Do they keep trying to change you?

15. Do they project their own disliked traits onto you?

16. Does the friendship exhaust you?

17. Do they drag you into their drama and mess?

18. What does your gut say?

Assess your answers to these questions. Do you have a toxic friend in tow? Sometimes, despite your best efforts to make a difficult friendship work, for your own mental well-being it has to end. Here are tips for cutting off someone who brings nothing to your life but negativity:

- Let go of the guilt. Pat yourself on the back for prioritising your emotional well-being.

- Talk in a public place to avoid a dramatic scene.

- Accept that it may be a process. If they don't respect your boundaries now, they may not after you cut them off.

- Don't argue. You're not trying to 'debate' the person into leaving you alone. This isn't a negotiation.

- Think about writing a letter. A letter is a sort of dress rehearsal for an in-person conversation. You can also refer back to the letter later, if you need to remember why you made the decision to cut someone out.

Use this space to write a letter to
your toxic friend, if you have one

SO, WHAT NOW?

We hope you feel inspired by this book and, most importantly, optimistic about your own future. Within these pages we know we didn't need to sugar-coat situations that many of you are already familiar with. But while things for us are still not by any means perfect, there has been progress, and we should acknowledge that the women we spoke to, and others like them, paved the way for us through a more difficult set of circumstances than we might be able to imagine today.

When Liz turned 21, and just after she had graduated, she wrote a note to herself about the approach she wanted to take in life. The note was a sort of promise, a manifesto that she could refer back to, that would reassure her whenever she lacked motivation, when a particular goal seemed impossible, when something she wanted didn't go to plan, or when someone let her down. A key part of this note was a quote from Maya Angelou: 'My mission in life is not merely to survive, but to thrive; and to do so with some passion, some compassion, some humour, and some style.'

Through ups and downs over the years Liz has gone back to this note and it has always reignited that spark in her, helping to refocus her purpose.

Write down your own note of reassurance that you can refer back to:

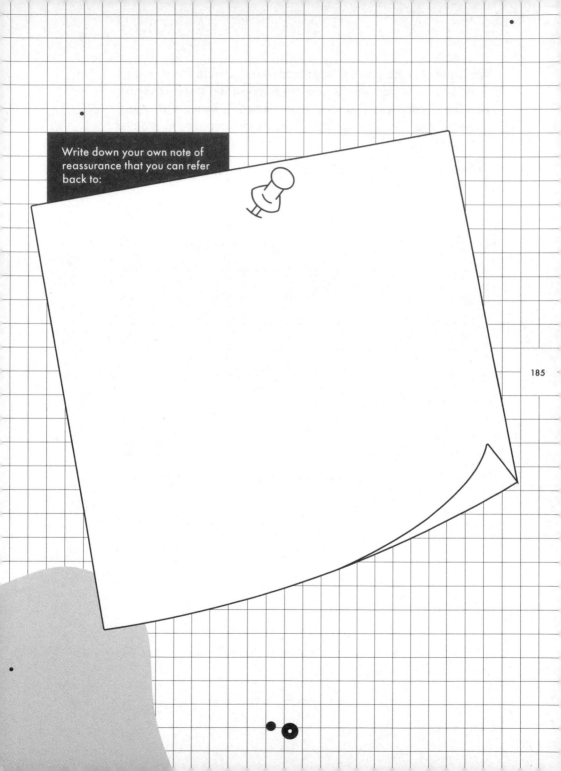

We hope that this journal does something similar for you, and that, depending on where you are in your life, it will reassure you that, whatever you may experience, whatever it is you have to offer the world, and whatever your purpose, you're not alone.

Write down ten things you have learnt about yourself on this journaling journey:

_____

_____

_____

_____

_____

_____

_____

_____

_____

Write down five tips for slaying in your lane that most struck a chord with you:

_____

_____

_____

_____

_____

Write down five things you hope to do differently from this point forward:

_____

_____

_____

_____

_____

Let's go back to your original definition of 'Slay In Your Lane' you wrote back in Chapter 1. Has your definition changed after everything you've learned on your journaling journey?

If so, what does *Slay In Your Lane* mean to you now? Write it down below:

_____

_____

_____

_____

_____

If you're comfortable doing so, share your thoughts and findings with your audience on social media so you can inspire them to slay in their own lanes!

WATER TRACKER

	MON.	TUE	WED.	THUR.	FRI.	SAT.	SUN.
Week 1	○○○○○ ○○○○○	○○○○○ ○○○○○	○○○○○ ○○○○○	○○○○○ ○○○○○	○○○○○ ○○○○○	○○○○○ ○○○○○	○○○○○ ○○○○○
Week 2	○○○○○ ○○○○○	○○○○○ ○○○○○	○○○○○ ○○○○○	○○○○○ ○○○○○	○○○○○ ○○○○○	○○○○○ ○○○○○	○○○○○ ○○○○○
Week 3	○○○○○ ○○○○○	○○○○○ ○○○○○	○○○○○ ○○○○○	○○○○○ ○○○○○	○○○○○ ○○○○○	○○○○○ ○○○○○	○○○○○ ○○○○○
Week 3	○○○○○ ○○○○○	○○○○○ ○○○○○	○○○○○ ○○○○○	○○○○○ ○○○○○	○○○○○ ○○○○○	○○○○○ ○○○○○	○○○○○ ○○○○○

SLEEP TRACKER

YEAR [...]   MONTH [...]

DAY	SLEEP DURATION	DREAMS
1	7 8 9 10 11 12 1 2 3 4 5 6 7 8 9 10 11 12 13	
2	7 8 9 10 11 12 1 2 3 4 5 6 7 8 9 10 11 12 13	
3	7 8 9 10 11 12 1 2 3 4 5 6 7 8 9 10 11 12 13	
4	7 8 9 10 11 12 1 2 3 4 5 6 7 8 9 10 11 12 13	
5	7 8 9 10 11 12 1 2 3 4 5 6 7 8 9 10 11 12 13	
6	7 8 9 10 11 12 1 2 3 4 5 6 7 8 9 10 11 12 13	
7	7 8 9 10 11 12 1 2 3 4 5 6 7 8 9 10 11 12 13	
8	7 8 9 10 11 12 1 2 3 4 5 6 7 8 9 10 11 12 13	
9	7 8 9 10 11 12 1 2 3 4 5 6 7 8 9 10 11 12 13	
10	7 8 9 10 11 12 1 2 3 4 5 6 7 8 9 10 11 12 13	
11	7 8 9 10 11 12 1 2 3 4 5 6 7 8 9 10 11 12 13	
12	7 8 9 10 11 12 1 2 3 4 5 6 7 8 9 10 11 12 13	
13	7 8 9 10 11 12 1 2 3 4 5 6 7 8 9 10 11 12 13	
14	7 8 9 10 11 12 1 2 3 4 5 6 7 8 9 10 11 12 13	
15	7 8 9 10 11 12 1 2 3 4 5 6 7 8 9 10 11 12 13	
16	7 8 9 10 11 12 1 2 3 4 5 6 7 8 9 10 11 12 13	
17	7 8 9 10 11 12 1 2 3 4 5 6 7 8 9 10 11 12 13	
18	7 8 9 10 11 12 1 2 3 4 5 6 7 8 9 10 11 12 13	
19	7 8 9 10 11 12 1 2 3 4 5 6 7 8 9 10 11 12 13	
20	7 8 9 10 11 12 1 2 3 4 5 6 7 8 9 10 11 12 13	
21	7 8 9 10 11 12 1 2 3 4 5 6 7 8 9 10 11 12 13	
22	7 8 9 10 11 12 1 2 3 4 5 6 7 8 9 10 11 12 13	
23	7 8 9 10 11 12 1 2 3 4 5 6 7 8 9 10 11 12 13	
24	7 8 9 10 11 12 1 2 3 4 5 6 7 8 9 10 11 12 13	
25	7 8 9 10 11 12 1 2 3 4 5 6 7 8 9 10 11 12 13	
26	7 8 9 10 11 12 1 2 3 4 5 6 7 8 9 10 11 12 13	
27	7 8 9 10 11 12 1 2 3 4 5 6 7 8 9 10 11 12 13	
28	7 8 9 10 11 12 1 2 3 4 5 6 7 8 9 10 11 12 13	
29	7 8 9 10 11 12 1 2 3 4 5 6 7 8 9 10 11 12 13	
30	7 8 9 10 11 12 1 2 3 4 5 6 7 8 9 10 11 12 13	
31	7 8 9 10 11 12 1 2 3 4 5 6 7 8 9 10 11 12 13	

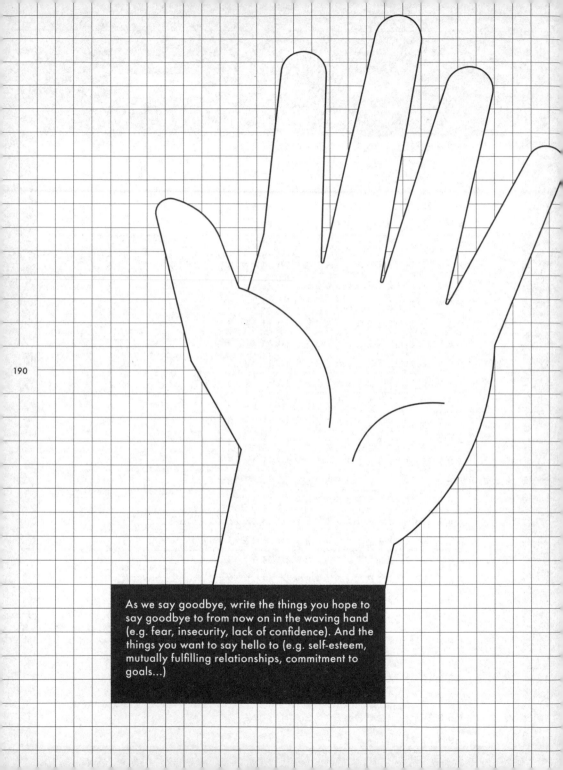

As we say goodbye, write the things you hope to say goodbye to from now on in the waving hand (e.g. fear, insecurity, lack of confidence). And the things you want to say hello to (e.g. self-esteem, mutually fulfilling relationships, commitment to goals...)

MY NOTES